MAGIC SOURCE CODES

THE CRAFT OF REALITY

CAT HOWELL

Cover photography by Haley Guildford

ISBN 978-0-473-65037-7

cathowell.com

Here's to falling into a deeply safe, thrilling, and loving relationship with yourself. And may you never fear a monster should you ever encounter one.

CONTENTS

PREFACE

It was time to put my plan into motion.

I'd sat patiently through dinner with my boyfriend and his family, but before dessert was even served, I get up to excuse myself.

He shoots me a confused and disappointed look as I begin saying my goodbyes.

Lately, there had been tension between us, although neither of us openly admitted it. The more I withheld from him, the more he withdrew from me. Such is the way these things go.

"I need to get some rest before my surgery tomorrow," I tell him. In reality, this was only partially true.

He hugs me goodbye, and I walk out to my car, get in, and let my shoulders sink thinking about my bed. But first, I have a stop I need to make.

Earlier that evening, I'd held my phone under the table so no one could see I was texting a friend.

I'm not winning this battle, do you have shrooms?

The answer I wanted came back.

Now, lights from the motorway cast shadows across my face.

I was tired.

I'd been having long days at work for what seemed like years now.

Pushing, pushing, always distracting. It was becoming unbearable. No matter how I looked at it, I always came back to the same sinking realization – it had to end now. Tomorrow would be the window.

As I stared down the roadway, I thought back to my boyfriend. To admit it all to him now would be to sacrifice losing too much, not a price I was prepared to pay.

I knew what had to be done.

A ding from my phone interrupts my thoughts.

I look down. There's a message from the medical center about my surgery. They want to make sure I'm ready for tomorrow and that I don't drink any liquids after 8pm.

I'd scheduled another breast augmentation. Another attempt in a long lineup of plastic surgeries to turn over the stone that would finally make me feel whole.

When I get newer, bigger boobs, then I will feel happy.

I knew I was grasping at straws, but this is where things had gotten to, desperation to the point of going under the knife.

The thing about life is that it isn't like the movies, there's no ominous swell of the music to let you know that you are veering off track. Instead, it's like a train silently changing rails in the middle of the night, a car turning onto an offramp. A reflection in a rearview mirror. A sleepy neighborhood.

Taking a deep breath, I park the car and walk up to my friend's front door. We'd been close when we were in uni, but had drifted apart in the past few years. Kids, life, things just got in the way.

She welcomes me inside and leads me into the kitchen - a space adorned in crystals, candles and macrame hangings across the walls. Her two young children are watching television in the other room and her husband is standing by the counter, staring intently at a gray-colored scale filled with mushrooms.

Psilocybin mushrooms, commonly known as magic mushrooms, contain the psychoactive chemical psilocin which leads to distortions of visuals, loss of perceptual time, sense of connectedness and heightened awareness. Enhanced wellbeing.

They think I'm here to cure myself.

"Can't I just take it by eye, like one shroom per day?" I ask him.

He scoffs. "Yea if you want to have a trip! It's better to measure these things as the goal is to microdose, not to get high."

"Here," he says, handing them over triumphantly after successfully squeezing them into a ziplock bag. His smile wilts as he sees my face and he pauses to collect his words, "You know, there's a lot of people that care about you."

I feel his eyes burrow through my soul.

Does he know? I wonder with a pang of guilt, it's my turn to look away embarrassed. He was concerned for my well-being and here I was deceiving him.

"I'll give you the money for it, just send me your account."

He raises both hands in objection, "It's for you, don't worry about it. You're so lucky we had some around when you asked."

I nod and hug them both goodbye.

Only four hours earlier, I had been searching online for the side effects of mixing anesthesia with mushrooms. It wasn't a good mix, or so the internet seemed to think.

Potentially fatal.

Perfect.

The disregard towards my own life had crossed new boundaries.

Thoughts chasing themselves like the fur scarves of older women.

Better to end this now. Kill the host, kill the virus.

Better to end this now than to endure another moment of the torture.

Better to end this now.

INTRODUCTION

"The All is mind, the universe is mental."

— *THE KYBALION*

One of the oldest spiritual texts in the world is the ancient Egyptian origin story of the Secret of Osiris Becoming Re. It tells of the ascension of Osiris into the sky and the creation of the physical universe from the flesh of Atum.[1]

Being the first god, Atum is said to have created himself by saying his own name. He first imagines himself and then, through his mouth, speaks himself into existence.

Depicted across sacred tombs and temples, illustrations tell of the creative cycle of life and death and the gods walking amongst us. Within us.

The hieroglyphic symbol represented as three seeds followed by a double helix and two raised arms denotes *hekau*, meaning "magic," defined as "words of power."

In Judaism, the *Torah* teaches that God created the world through ten utterances and that humans were gifted with this capacity for divine speech. "Through the word of God, the heavens were made; and through the breath of His mouth, all of their hosts." (Psalms 33:6)

In Buddhism, this is told as, "What you think, you become. What you feel, you attract. What you imagine, you create."

In esotericism, "Abracadabra": "I create as I speak."

ABRACADABRA
ABRACADABR
ABRACADAB
ABRACADA
ABRACAD
ABRACA
ABRAC
ABRA
ABR
AB
A

Abracadabra is a 2nd century word of power that was inscribed across triangular amulets worn to ward off sickness.

What we say, and more importantly, how we say it and how often we say it, matters. "Death and life are in the tongue."[2]

Through our words, we enchant reality. Through our hands, we mold intentions. Through our bodies, we transmute energy. Through our thoughts, we invoke action.

And in this way, we are complicit magicians. Always engaged in the act of magic, always enchanting ourselves, whether we know it or not.

The human body is the ultimate magic wand.

But while it appears the ancients understood this, we have never really been told this.

Instead, we are bred and led to believe that the physical reality is the real truth of how things are, that technology is just science and that our ability to change the physical is mostly achieved through hard work and action.

Some of us are even made to fear our creative capacities and intuitions and most of us only know how to engage magic intentionally through the technologies we use. Technology that helps us to control, harness, and manage the information field around us to heal, grow, learn, and change perspectives. All day. Every day.

Normalized to such an extent that we cannot see it for what it is.

But, if you were to tell an early human trying to find their way back home that in the twenty-first century we use microwave frequencies to navigate the globe (GPS), they would call this magic.

If you were to tell an ancient Egyptian trying to evoke a loved one that, these days, we can video call someone across the world with virtually no lag, they would also call this magic.

Back then, the Mesolithic shaman used divination techniques to predict weather systems and fertility. These days, we use wi-fi radio waves to search Google...

Back then, incantations and voices were used to heal the body. These days, we use high-frequency ultrasound waves to cure cancer…

And while shamanism is a practice dating back over 27,000 years and the earliest known profession, alchemy and the world of magic have been mostly blacklisted and classified in modern culture under themes of horror and sci-fi.

Tools and techniques that were once widely used and adopted by our ancestors were vilified and warned against. Emotions were mocked, and enchantments became heresy. For who are we to try to alter "divine intent"?

The Library of Alexandria, which contained an estimated 400,000 scrolls and the works of Greek philosophers such as Plato, Aristotle, and Pythagoras as well as sacred hermetic and magical texts was the most comprehensive library of ancient times. It was all but gone within a few centuries, burned to rubble, and replaced by mosques and churches. Such was the breadth of scientific knowledge housed within the library that it is often speculated that – were it not for the destruction of this great repository – humanity may not have fallen into the Dark Ages that followed the fall of Rome.

Over the centuries to come, practitioners of alchemy were hunted down and burned at the stake. Wizards and shamans were forced into the shadows.

Thankfully, many other ancient documents survived the hands of time, all hinting back to the creative capacities within.

In the 1500-year-old Coptic texts found at Nag Hammadi dating back further than the New Testament, Jesus is recorded as saying:

"If you bring forth what is within you, what you bring forth will save you. If you do not bring forth what is within you, what you do not bring forth will destroy you."

Which begs the question, what is within you, and do you know how to bring it forth?

And, if – already within us – is the capacity to invent technologies of everyday magic, does this not make us inherently more capable and powerful than those devices?

What if, as Wayne Dyer says, all that exists was once imagined and all that will exist is now being imagined?

What if we are a creative force, intended to fulfill and "bring forth" an expression of desires?

What if in every single word uttered from our lips exists a universe of infinite probabilities?

For most of my adult life, I used to think that magic was something purely to entertain children with. Charlatanism and sleight of hand.

This attitude existed despite the fact that I was knee deep in manifestation and Law of Attraction concepts, I had experienced the power of intention, and had an active daily mindfulness practice.

I refused to believe in magic purely because science could not prove it irrefutably. But, if magic is measured in terms of synchronicities (meaningful coincidences) and meaning is subjective to the perceiver. Then, synchronicity is relative and not something that could ever truly be proven.

For example, back in 2018 I was printing and selling t-shirts for my advertising company with the slogan "I'm a Facebook Marketer, Not a F**king Magician!". At that time, I was beginning to feel the ebb of a growing depression taking over and was in dire need of help. If you would have told me just five years ago that the very first book I would come to put to print – after a lifetime of yearning to be a published author – would be on the topic of magic and that it would be magic that would help pull me out from the depression, I would have laughed you out of the room. That I would make a literal one-eighty flip since then is both a testament to the delicious irony of life and the trouble with trying to pin down magic, which can occur laterally across a timeframe that makes it easy to miss.

And so magic requires both acute perception of synchronicities and blind trust going in. You are the only one who will be able to irrefutably prove its existence.

Photo of merchandise I had commissioned in 2018 for my company – just one example of a "meaningful synchronicity" that makes magic difficult to pin down fully.

In this way, the journey of magic is one that always leads us back to ourselves. It is the understanding that even the smallest seeds, planted in thought or soil, can grow into the grandest of oaks.

That magic has persisted, despite all the best efforts to suppress it throughout the ages, is a testament not only to its resilience in thought leadership, but also its efficacy. Occam's Razor stipulates that it is ineradicable because there is merit to its validity.

This book is a literal manifestation of magic and the creative expression of what is "within me", born on the back of deep resistance I encountered in my business and trusting myself through the fog.

It is a meditation on the spiritual nature of the creative process, an examination of age-old concepts and how these can be applied within the modern-day context.

My hope is to inspire you to understand the wand that is you and to provide you with techniques and practical guidance on how to begin to recreate the rules of your own reality using the altar within.

It is an enchantment back into a remembering space of yourself, an expansion in perception of meaning. A rediscovery of the creative core and of the vast capacities within.

As you read the contents, I encourage you to modify and adapt what is shared to suit your needs. As you will come to understand, magic is a narration of a story we tell ourselves and the best stories are the ones we are eager to tell. Create a practice that excites and compels you. Approach magic with an open heart and have fun with it.

And so, with that, begins our journey together into the rabbit hole, as you dive in, I invite you to access additional training and resources at magicsourcecodes.com/training.

Here is to your journey and success.

Cat

Always Forgetting

You will forget this moment in time

Ten cycles of the moon from now

...the worry will seem all but a distant memory

A moment in time when it felt impossible

When the odds were stacked against you

When you didn't think you'd make it through

Because at this moment in time, you had come to forget other moments in time

When you felt the same

When you believed the same

And yet...

And yet...

Here you are

You always made it through

And in ten moon cycles from now

...when the circumstances once more feel like dysfunction

You will be forgetting about today's gray

Because here you are

Always forgetting just how powerful you really are

1

HOW WE GOT HERE

"You should never make decisions based on emotions."

These words kept repeating in my head as I drove to my downtown office.

My sister had surprised me by giving me a session with a human design specialist as a "hope you get better" gift. This was just one in a long line of therapists I'd seen recently.

My mind kept drifting back to our session. The specialist, a woman in her forties who wore a red scarf around her neck, pulled up a screen that looked like squiggles etched across the form of a human body. I couldn't make any sense of it. As she traced the colored lines with her cursor, she nodded her head as if agreeing with herself. Her right eyebrow raised as if to say, *See?*

But what I saw was just squiggles. I did not see.

But I heard, and what I heard was, "Quit the business." To be fair, she never actually said those words; it was an inner voice that decided to dub her out.

And even though the session I had just had was the inspiration for what I was about to do, the seed had been planted long ago.

Just two weeks earlier, right after the breast augmentation surgery, my world had come crashing down around me.

After two years of hiding a depression from everyone, it had all come out in the open – like an ugly muffin top – the day my boyfriend's friend and colleague was shot dead on the job in a freak incident.

Mental breakdown.

And when it first came spilling out, it was the most unflattering of affairs.

My suicidal confession landed right after my boyfriend broke up with me. He told me I'm not the one. I responded by saying I wanted to kill myself. Classy.

I could say I had been building up the courage to tell him all along, but deep down, I knew I had said it to make him stay.

He fearfully called my friends and I was promptly placed on suicide watch with those around me taking shifts to sleep over and hold my hand.

I was mortified, heartbroken, and depressed.

But now, two weeks after the breakup, a two-week absence from the business, and two weeks of settling into a new normal where friends and family text at random hours of the day just to check in, now there was a new spark of encouragement from the human design specialist. I was sure that resigning would be the key to it all.

With almost one hundred percent certainty, I suspected the business was responsible for what was happening. Quitting would be the solution to make it all come right.

I pulled into the parking garage and took a deep breath, trying to stop all the thoughts racing inside my head. In my hand, I held a small piece of paper containing words I knew I would want to remember once I got inside.

Time to go, I told myself.

I got out of the car and walked into the office. I looked around the room, seeing how I'd set everything up just the way I'd planned on my vision board. For years, I had obsessed over this space and now, here it was; it no longer seemed relevant.

Instead of heading to my desk, I asked everyone to gather around.

My team huddled around me, some sitting in chairs. Others sat on the edge of desks. I could tell they were wondering if this would be a celebratory catch-up or the "you're all fired" kind of meeting.

I cleared my throat and felt myself choke up, already fighting back the tears. I just knew I would dissolve the moment anyone said a word.

"Ummm…"

I wasn't sure how to break the news.

My fingers twisted around the small piece of paper. The words I hadn't wanted to forget were now rendered pulped mush from the grip of my sweaty hands. I was on my own.

I hadn't exactly planned this out. I had only decided three hours earlier. My team, here now, looked back at me with dread etched across their faces.

Standing before them, about to deliver the news I knew I had to, suddenly, the burst of inspiration that had come from the human design specialist seemed to fizzle out.

Fuck! I'm supposed to be the leader, the responsible one. What am I doing?

"As... Ummm..."

I sputtered the words out and needed to swallow my spit before they could come out properly.

"As effective immediately," I tried to level my voice, "I am resigning as CEO." I continued, distending my sentences to help me overcome the buildup of tears. "As of today, you will need to learn to run this business without me." I nodded and tried to plaster the news with some optimism and a half-hearted smile, but snot was beginning to form in my nose.

There, I said it. I did the dirty deed that needed doing.

They all looked back, shocked and mildly confused. Is this a joke? Big eyes blinking. It was clear from the fat silence that hung in the air no one wanted to utter a word lest it makes it all true. My face looked broken. I was serious. They searched each other's gazes in confusion. They wanted more. It was all so sudden and out of nowhere.

"I'm on the verge of killing myself," I clarified, choking up. "I need to take time to figure things out." The least I could do was give them the truth. They had deserved the truth a long time ago, but here we were.

The tears that had been building rolled down my cheek, and snot began to run out my nose, which I awkwardly wiped with the back of my sleeve. The pandemic had just hit a few months back, and exposed bodily fluids weren't exactly crowd favorites. A hand reached out and handed me a tissue.

I was thirty-three years old, and depression had slipped into my life in the same way that the taproot of a plant unfurls below ground – slowly, unnoticed until one day it's a thick and twisted trunk that strangles out all the light.

I had caught the scent of a monster.

Even though I had everything I could have ever dreamed of – a successful multimillion-dollar business, industry accolades, followers, beautiful, healthy children, a new house, and a new car – something rotten had taken over inside like a parasite.

Inside my mind, it felt like the hijacked cockroach that walked into the hungry pupa's den. Something not of me had taken over me.

I had made millions, conquered the mountain, flexed my forearm, and drove in the stake...

And then…

I realized, with a dropping smile, that there were even more peaks, even bigger mountains. It would never end. I was never satisfied. It's like the study where millionaires are asked if they are happy, and the answers are always "no" regardless of their income level.

I asked myself, *was this the machine I wanted to be a part of?*

Detachment. From there, it was a slippery slope, a circuit, so to speak.

I feared losing the things that I had. I feared losing my partner. I feared losing my identity. I feared losing the inner-city office. But most of all, I feared the meaning I would attach to losing everything.

I slipped into a quicksand of confusion and cynicism. The more I tried to fix things, the more burdensome it all became.

All I could see were more murky puddles and sandstorms. A bottomless pit where nothing is filled or satisfied for long. The trips had to be more extravagant, the partying more extreme, and the hits stronger and stronger each time just to sustain a flatline in my mind.

A moth with wet wings.

The first sign of the rot, of the monster's scent, had been the wilting of the plants around me.

When I moved the team into the office space, it had been a quarter of its size. I dreamt of creating a production studio, so I convinced the landlord to tear down walls and build me a grand old space.

To celebrate the expansion, I threw a big party and spent thousands decorating the new space with plants. I wanted a jungle and purchased glorious palms in big white pots and cacti reaching out to the concrete vaulted ceilings. I hung spider ivy and various perennials to give the impression of a wall where there was none as if one were living under a willow.

The night of the party, once everyone had left, my boyfriend and I had fucked in one of the empty rooms furnished only with a rug. My knees blistered and bled, but neither one of us had noticed.

I would find myself staying late in the office by myself a lot, long after the sun had already fallen behind the tall concrete towers. Sitting on the windowsill of the meeting room, looking down at the grey mass of buildings and dots of back-lit windows, little figures occupying tiny match-stick apartments; office workers staying late under fluorescent lights, blowing smoke through the small gap in the window into the city night. Nothing but the whir of the rolling security camera in the corner to keep me company.

I was too consumed with the monster in my head to notice all the plants were dying around me, begging to be saved. I guess plants move at a slower pace of life, a different time dimension. Their deaths can be easy to miss.

When everyone in the office did start to notice the botanical plight, all hands were on deck to save them. We assigned strict watering schedules, which initially seemed to perk them up, but nothing worked for long. We would change their positions around the space, thinking maybe the light was the problem, but the office was brightly lit. We scratched our heads, wondering what was going on.

And then, I also realized somewhere along the line, the plants in my house had started to do the same. Brown and furl upon themselves. I wasn't sure how long it had been going on, but there seemed to be mimicry happening.

Mimicry between the plants and my own mental headspace, all of it wilting.

It was around this time that the chaos started to show up more and more in my life. Like the sadistic torture chamber of the little emerald wasp, I was made to watch as I took myself down, piece by piece. I wanted to jump in and help the girl before me, but when I opened my mouth, only air came out, and when I went to hug her, my arms glitched in a circuit of time, never arriving.

To add to the mess of it all, Covid had hit a few months before. Lockdowns were happening across the globe, and the movie *Contagion* was making the rounds. I walked around in a constant state of hijacked fear.

As I sat in the office confessing to my mental state, my team and I hugged each other and cried together.

At that moment, I was prepared to lose the business. Lose all that I had acquired. It had become a matter of life or death. The office no longer mattered.

I felt a weight lift, even if only momentarily.

Things can only go up from here, I told them all with a half-hearted chuckle.

As I took the elevator back down that afternoon and walked across the street into a tiny bookstore, I didn't know that this day was not even close to my rock bottom and that I would soon come to lose so much more.

Inside the store, I walked up to a shelf stacked with non-fiction books. Now that I was officially "unemployed," I felt like a drifter and the bookstore like the temporary wedge between what had been and what would be. I picked out a hardcover book at random and cracked its spine open.

Glaring back at me on the page was the word "QUIT". It read: "Of all the best strategies, knowing when to quit may be the best."

2

MONSTER

The word monster comes from the Latin *monere,* meaning "to warn." It can also be traced back to *monstrum,* as in "divine omen." Divine as in "of god" or "good" and omen as in "event of prophetic significance."

And so, a monster is both a blessing and a warning. It will cover your face in kisses before ripping off your head – if you catch my drift.

Omen.

Usually, the feeling of confusion is one of the first signs that a monster is on your tail. It will start to eat you up from the inside. Contracting, expanding, billowing clouds of question marks.

It feels somewhat soothing and intoxicating, like a flame burning away grime. Smoke in the lungs.

"Look into my eyes," the monster will say.

When you do, it will take hold of your system, like a code interjecting circuits, like the emerald wasp injecting poison into a cockroach's brain.

This is what a monster does.

Parasitism, using you purely for habitat and resources.

And once it gets a scent, it won't matter where you run or how many demons you try to exorcize. Fancy trips will only buy you so much time.

It will chase you down until there is nothing left of you. Just a puffed-out brown shell of what you once were.

Until you are no longer choosing yourself.

The omen, of course, is that if you make it out alive, you're stronger for it.

It was this monster that led me into the cave of the magical treasure of alchemy. Like *Ali Baba and the Forty Thieves,* I yelled out "*Open Sesame!*" and the monster became my own enchantment. The word sesame is from Hebrew *šem* for God.

Of course, the cave didn't just open, the monster didn't just move out of the way, and the magic wasn't instantly perceptible.

The taproot had sunk in, and the monster's curved beak had already begun to chew on the buttered parts of my mind.

And so, there was a struggle and there was chaos.

Omen.

3

THE CHAOS THAT EXISTS

"The positive cannot exist without the negative, you only know what to be by contrast of what not to be."

ALAN WATTS

Seth, the god of chaos in ancient Egyptian mythology, was both worshiped and despised. He controlled the desert, weather storms, and all things natural and violent.

On the other hand, his brother Osiris was revered and praised as a pillar of Egypt who blessed the land with bountiful harvests and just laws.

Seth became jealous of his brother's rule and plotted to usurp his throne, luring Osiris to his death and cutting him into fourteen pieces, which he then scattered throughout Egypt.

Isis, the widow of Osiris and mother of magic, searched across the dunes and swamps of the Nile for the pieces of her lost love and found all but one. Undeterred, she brewed a potion to return him to eternal life, where he descended to the underworld to rule the afterlife.

The cutting up of Osiris into fourteen parts is as much a story of family dysfunction as it is a testament to the process of change and motion as the only true constants of our universe – death and life and the laws of duality.

Just as the true power of the seed lies in receiving sunlight after being planted in the dark, acts of creation exist in a constant tension between opposing desires and thought. Disorder and order.

Dissolution and decay give way to rebirth and transformation, in much the same way that the snake sheds its skin, a tadpole becomes a frog, or how the rotting trunk of the mother log gives sustenance to the growing saplings and universes of insects.

Everything is in a flux of reinvention. The process of creativity involves both separation and unification. Nothing in life is ever permanent, it's all backwashed recycling, from stardust to styrofoam cup.

To plant the seed, both in soil and mind, is to engage in this unending cycle of regeneration – a serpent with its tail in its mouth, a figure eight forever looping.

To be conscious is to be compelled towards this unending cycle and it is only when we allow ourselves to live truly from this creative core that we find fulfillment and contentment.

No one can choose to opt out of this process because we are literal manifestations of it, a physical vessel to experience creation on the nonphysical plane. A start and an end.

Pretending a world where only heaven or positivity deserve to exist is to plunge ourselves into resistance where chaos serves as a mechanism to help us transcend.

Because it is in losing our job that we go on to start our own projects. It is the cancer scare that inspires a spark for life. It is a loss that gives an appreciation for what we have and it is the heartbreak that delivers us to our true match.

In the *Buddha and the Badass,*[1] Vishen describes these moments of disorder as *kensho moments,* experiences so disruptive and unsettling that they lift the dust in such a way that when it settles back down, one is never quite the same again.

And so, the practice of alchemy, more than anything, is a practice of seeing oneself through both the yin and the yang, of respecting the right for co-creative forces to exist.

Empedocles, the great Greek philosopher, once said love always follows strife. Evolution happens through mutilation and breakage. Life cannot be sustained without the other. Just as the cosmos always follows chaos.

Duality, attraction, and repulsion is the underlying process of magic.

And while we cannot escape this powerful creative force of chaos, we can change how we respond to it. By allowing it the right to exist and move through our lives, we transmute it into expansive growth.

Because we are ultimately creative beings, the force of expansion.

And what we discover is that when we are calibrated to our creative cores, when we are intentionally crafting from the unknown, we minimize chaos existing in our lives. We no longer attract it as much for the simple reason that we no longer require it to remember ourselves. We are already aligned to our own path of least resistance.

Of course, none of this I understood as I watched the monster take over my own life.

I couldn't see the invitation to see myself once more.

All I perceived was the attack and the pain associated with it.

At first, the chaos started showing up as things breaking down around me; technology, computers, agreements, and plants dying. This led to a healthy amount of frustration.

Gradually building up momentum, I began losing clients. Sales started declining. Revenues flatlined. I saw my relationships crumble in front of me. My trust was betrayed by others. Many nights, I'd wake up in cold sweats from anxiety.

The more I tried to fix things, the more I seemed to feed the beast until the ultimate betrayal took place – a ransom on my own head, placed by yours truly.

All I saw around me was loneliness, desperation, the stupidness of myself

I became cynical, and every financial and romantic setback felt like a signal that I should just erase myself.

I couldn't see that I was no longer rooted in my own creative core.

And so, in this way, I had come to lose my own mind so that I could find it once more.

Incantation — Transmuting Chaos

An incantation is a series of formulated words strung together for magical intent and is the original practice of affirmations used by ancient Egyptian priests and priestesses.

The Latin word *incantare*, which means "to consecrate with spells," forms the basis of the word "enchant."

And while the major monotheistic religions of Islam, Judaism, and Christianity have labeled incantations as immoral and evil, it is argued that prayer is a form of this practice and certainly ancient Babylonian and Assyrian texts indeed seem to consider this to also be the case.[2]

At the core of the incantation is speech, or the magical word. How the words are strung together is just as important as what is actually said. In *Coral Gardens and their Magic* (1935), Bronisław Malinowski suggests that "the knowledge of the right words, appropriate phrases and the more highly developed forms of speech, gives man a power over and above his own limited field of personal action."

To transform a simple intention or affirmation into a magical incantation, write out what it is you would like to intend.

For example, let's say you are also facing chaos or dysfunction in your life, which you would like to transmute, you could write the phrase:

"These recent experiences of chaos are now transmuted into expansion and transformation, serving me for the greater good."

Saying and repeating this sentence aloud to yourself is a typical method of affirmation. But to make it even more compelling, try to alter the words to create rhythm and rhyme.

For example, the original phrase could be turned into:

"This moment of chaos I now undo,

All that was changed return anew."

It can be helpful to search for the root meaning of words to craft even more powerful incantations.

I often like to listen to chanting or isochronic music while reciting the phrase to help deepen focus and gnosis (more on gnosis in later chapters).

As the magician, you are the one who gets to narrate and write your story. You are the one who enchants yourself.

Use this moment now to set the intention of what you would like to transmute and create an incantation of it.

If you are unclear yet about what the intent should be, have fun with this exercise and call to yourself a moment of synchronicity. Something that will hold much meaning for you when it shows up in your life.

Only attempt this exercise when you are in a relatively good head space and mood.

4

SUICIDE

The human design specialist was wrong, I thought to myself as I pulled out the letters and neatly lined them side by side on the table. Some were smeared in blue ink and blots of tears. It had taken me nearly three hours to write them all. My hand had cramped for the rest of the day. They were repurposed from the last attempt.

I'm so sorry, I can't do it anymore some of the letters say.

Earlier that week, a holistic healer I'd seen had told me my throat chakra was blocked and that I needed to better communicate my desires and needs – even if only to myself.

To help unblock my chakra, he instructed me to scream into salt water. So I took myself down to the beach, zipped up my wetsuit, and waded out into the cold waves, dunking my head in the water and letting out a scream that came out in bubbles.

With my head under the water, my mind began to cycle images. I remembered my ex fucking me, saw his head between my legs, the night it got sloppy, the walls scrawled in sticky notes that said things like "THINK OF THE KIDS!" or "He'll come back." I saw the countdown scribbled over in the journal, the tattoos on the knuckles, the dog looking at me as I unpacked a helium tank I'd ordered online.

I did what the holistic healer suggested, but it didn't seem to make any difference. In fact, things in my life were getting progressively worse. I was more confused and depressed than before I had quit. Now, I was almost positive I'd really lost the plot. I had been so sure that walking away from the business would have suddenly made everything come right. I hadn't even thought out what would happen if I'd been wrong.

My life was spiraling off in a direction without propulsion, and I watched helplessly as the things I had spent years building began crumbling around me.

I could no longer sustain the mortgage of the million-dollar city home. I needed to downgrade. I was still torn from the heartbreak, with a knife in my heart.

And so, I spent most of my days just sleeping, half in and out of bed, blue Gatorade bottles leading a trail around the house.

A growing itch to erase building, a scratching frustration at the mirror. Lockdowns and separation left me alone with the monster in my head.

Burn it at the stake.

That's the dangerous thing about depression. It gives you tunnel vision and locks you into the most dramatic solution. It undermines the creative capacities.

I didn't know how I would ever feel well again. It didn't feel like I would ever heal.

I wrote in my journal:

What if, for some people, the real world just doesn't feel right anymore? Surely it's better for everybody if those people just stay out of the way?

That's how it felt inside.

Slumped in my bed, floating like a double-chinned sea otter, I asked myself, *Is this God?*

I pulled the plastic bag and CPAP mask over my head and turned on the helium tank. According to what I had read on the internet, I should be dead within a few minutes.

The branch of a magnolia tree scratched at the window.

I could smell the gas. My pulse began to rise, caused by a panic that I needed to actively quell. It was just my biological being going into survival circuits. I had to override it. The smell burned in the lungs.

Calm down, I told myself as I felt my breath quicken in alarm.

And just then, there was a firm knock on the door.

It startled me. The bag holding the helium gas opened, releasing it into the air. I scrambled to turn off the bottle as the knock came once more, this time more urgently.

Knock, knock, knock!

I stuffed the bottle and bag inside my closet, quickly collected all the neatly lined suicide letters, and placed them in a cupboard.

Sometimes, when magic shows up, it is in the form of divine timing.

5

REFLECTIONS

When i hit the rock bottom
That exists after the rock bottom
And no rope or hand appeared
i wondered
what if nothing wants me
because i do not want me
i am both the poison and the antidote

— RUPI KAUR

Have you ever heard of the story of Rainbow Girl?

She wasn't so much a girl as a creature of botany, with roots instead of legs.

She lived in a big, beautiful home with all the finest trimmings that money could buy. Around her were acres of beautiful gardens, mazes of opulence and all of the friends and success one could ever desire.

But Rainbow Girl wasn't happy.

You see, she was a potted plant and potted plants can never escape the frustration of their own compressed root balls – looping around like a nest of suffocation.

Potted plants can never touch the grime of thick decay belowground and can only daydream of shattering through their terracotta prisons, and even then, this freedom is seldom afforded. A root that has never been allowed to grow in girth is hardly a worthy opponent to a solid pot.

Besides, Rainbow Girl reasoned with herself, if she even so happened to free herself from the cradle, what then? How would she even survive such exposure to the elements?

Some things are better left a fantasy.

So instead, Rainbow Girl suffered silently and smiled diligently at all the beautiful things being paraded in front of her, all the while her leaves browned and withered, falling around her.

Look, they all cheered, *look at all that you have, look at how great it all is!*

But she could not muster herself to perk up, there had been a taste of something more and one she could no longer ignore.

Then, one day, a great big storm blew through. It flooded all of the land, everything submerged under water until there were no more but little floating islands of rooftops and hilltops.

Her porcelain pot was smashed during the flood, and currents tore at her roots.

She felt herself rip apart, she felt it all – the storm, the lightning, the searing of herself. The deafening silence that comes from the ringing call of death.

She was sure she was no longer alive, chaos flashed around her, blackness swallowed her whole.

But gradually, slowly, the waters subsided, and Rainbow Girl washed up in a new space she did not know. Her roots hung limp about her.

She felt deeply broken in ways she had never experienced before. Bruised beyond yellow. But the skies stilled and turned to blue, and the sun began to shine once more.

Slowly, there was an awakening, a remembering, and a tapping.

Her roots – at first hesitant – sunk into fresh, rich soil, padding deeper into new humus.

Fresh leaves began to unfurl, bigger than before and – now – streaked with a strange pink streak, like a magician's ribbon.

Rainbows began to end where she grew, casting prisms over her. When the rainbows shone, everyone around her saw them too.

They did not know what to call her and so they named her Rainbow Girl.

Brrriiiiinnnnnnggggggg

"How do you feel now?" they asked her, their words sounding more like blurred-out trumpets.

Like a Rainbow Girl! I know they can't hear me. The words are not words but air caught in my throat.

"What do you see now?" Their voices make me want to laugh. Do they even know how ridiculous they sound? Waddyyuooooo seeeeee naaaaaaaaeeeeeeoooowwwww?

Rainbows. Just rainbows. I try to reach out to them, to show them my broken roots but my arms feel ledden.

Brrriiiiinnnnnnggggggg, my alarm went off, the dream dissipated into something that felt difficult to pin down.

The room came into blurred focus as my eyelids struggled to open against crusted mascara. *No, no, no, no!* I scrambled inside. I was still alive.

Rainbow Girl no more.

This had been the morning routine for some months now. I would wake up and act surprised I was still alive, and then fall into my depressed self for the day.

Annoyed that I had woken up yet another morning, I fumbled at my phone. The sickening rise of a mother of all hangovers and the smell of the beer bottles next to me made my stomach hurl.

The knock at the door had been my personal assistant checking in on me. Oblivious to the hidden tank and suicide letters, she made me promise I would not harm myself and when she left, I had gotten blind drunk in shame instead.

Now alive, defeated, and confused, I crawled out of bed and emptied the contents of my stomach in the toilet.

I covered my face with my hoodie, masking blotchy crescents of mascara under my eyes. My hair was a static tangle. My head hurt, my eyes were swollen, and my bones ached. I wanted to pick at the seam of an invisible hole, like the broken lining of a purse where things get lost, never to be found again.

There is little more depressing than failing to kill yourself.

Fuck.

I spent the rest of the day lying in the fetal position, milking an energy drink. My head was pounding and memories from the previous day came back as flashes.

I'd had enough. I'd touched the bottom of the bottom and reached the density of a single particle, vibrating itself into a frenetic state. The only way out was to explode outwards again.

Blah.

There is no magic here.

Later that night, I was sitting in my drug dealer's car feeling silly that I had to even sit in the car like I was a criminal beneath the streetlights for a bag of weed. I needed to numb my mind.

Along the quiet and empty street lined bumper to bumper with cars, I could see the yellow glow of my living room across the road. It looked warm and inviting, but I knew what was waiting inside. Those letters and a stuffy bedroom of unwashed sheets filled with the air of something sick.

I wasn't in the mood to talk.

My dealer, a young guy in his twenties wearing a red hoodie, frowned when he saw my face. I guess I looked like a ghost.

"You ok?" he asked, handing me the bag of weed. His car was littered with receipts and empty food packets.

"Yea, just going through some stuff," I mumbled, counting out the money and handing it over.

"You know…" I tensed up. His hands hovered as he grabbed the money. *Just grab it*, I thought to myself, but he paused and continued, "When I was going through my existential crises, I realized that everything bad happening in my life was just a reflection of me."

I took the bag and thanked him, my lips in a straight line. I got out of the car and closed the door behind me. As I crossed the dark, empty street, I heard his car pull out and drive off. The sounds of the city hummed low in the background.

His comment bothered me in the way that a clothing tag hanging from a top does. It was like an important message that was only half revealed – like the scratched remembrance that you left the stove on back home.

What did a twenty-year-old know of existential crises? I scoffed as I entered the house.

Was he insinuating all the shit happening was my fault? The depression. The monster, the confusion, the heartbreak?

The whole thing reeked of toxic positivity.

There was a strong urge to defend myself. But to whom exactly I wasn't sure. None of it mattered now, anyway. I hadn't given up on suicide. It was my backup plan.

As soon as life throws in one more curveball, I told myself, *I will be gone.* Somehow, knowing this seemed to take the edge off.

I smoked a big joint and passed out.

The In-Between

No one ever talks about the in-between part…

Where you're no longer the caterpillar but not yet the butterfly.

A non-thing, formless and nameless. Every fiber of your body aching to transform, become something else, transcend into disruption.

You don't yet know who you are.

And you are no longer what you were.

Trapped inside old skin with a desire to stretch wings that have not yet formed.

The world is turbulent, from this angle, no doubt.

Fighting urges to melt back into the known.

But this is not the death of you.

It is merely the death of who you once were.

This is rebirth.

Transformation that comes from chaos.

So, surrender. Breakdown.

Stretch into the discomfort as you shed the past.

Fall to pieces if you need to.

For tomorrow, my darling, tomorrow the monarch will rise again.

6

BURN AT THE STAKE

For, where God built a church there the Devil would also build a chapel.

MARTIN LUTHER

For many, the word "witch" is synonymous to pacts with the devil, pointy black hats, and haggard old women standing over boiling cauldrons of chopped-up children. For centuries, the term was used to derogatively describe a malicious outlier of society (typically female), who used magic for evil intent.

But this was not always the case. Ancient Sumerians regarded witches as seers and diviners who played a crucial role in society and the "witch" personification was present in early China, Babylon, and Egypt. Common folk widely believed in witchcraft and people would buy and sell magical services like love potions and spells to help find stolen belongings. It was an acceptable profession and even tolerated by early Christians.

In fact, between 900 and 1400, Christian authorities were unwilling to even admit witches existed, let alone try someone for the crime of being one, and in 1258 Pope Alexander IV issued a canon to prevent prosecutions for witchcraft.[1] The Lombard code of 643 states: *Let nobody presume to kill a foreign serving maid or female servant as a witch, for it is not possible, nor ought to be believed by Christian minds.*

This all changed by 1550 when a political Catholic-Protestant tug-of-war for confessionals led Christian authorities to reverse their position entirely. At this time, witches existed in droves, and to protect citizens against the perilous threat witchcraft posed to their safety and well-being, it was recommended that they should all be prosecuted and punished wherever they were found.[2]

Prosecutors declared that witches allied themselves with the devil and this anti-diabolism preaching was used as a tool of propaganda in a bid to win religious market share, in much the same way that contemporary Republican and Democrat candidates focus campaign activity on a scapegoat during elections to attract the loyalty of undecided voters.

And it worked, the result was a literal witch hunt ensuing across Christendom with witches the easy target in the Catholic and Protestant Counter-Reformation confessional battleground.

In the wake of this 'Great Hunt', which lasted roughly 150 years, an estimated 80,000-120,000 people were tried for witchcraft and half were brutally executed.

More than 80 percent of those accused were women. Typically willful females who were independent professionals, healers, and midwives. The fear of female power often targeted elderly women who were marginal in society because they had often lost the oversight of male kin and their reproductive role after menopause.

In 1608, the puritan William Perkins published *Discourse on the Damned Art of Witchcraft* where he outlined the key indications that someone was indeed a witch. According to Perkins, if you experienced misfortune after having a quarrel with someone, it was likely that you had been cursed. This work became a standard text on the topic of witches in the English-speaking world at the time.

Mass executions occurred on both sides of the Atlantic.

Perhaps most notable of them all is the Salem trials which reached unprecedented heights and led to nearly 10% of the small Massachusetts town's population being accused of witchcraft!

It all started one day in 1692 when two young girls fell mysteriously ill.

At the time, the town was under the constant threat of Native American attacks and smallpox, and young women, whose primary role in society was to find a suitable husband, were under constant pressure to comply.

The two young girls lived with their father, a local preacher, and the family Arawak Indian slave Tituba, who had been purchased in Barbados.

It was a favorite pastime of the young girls to indulge in the divination practice of cracking an egg into a glass and interpreting what they saw. And on one such instance, the girls claimed to have foreseen a coffin in the egg.

Not long after, both girls entered violent fits and bouts of screaming.

The local doctor was called in but he could only scratch his head in puzzlement and soon this mysterious affliction spread to five other girls in the town. Unable to diagnose or prescribe the condition, the doctor chalked it down to the devil.

Upon this declaration, the Reverend and his family promptly set about baking a "witch cake," a cake made of rye mixed with the girls' urine, which would supposedly reveal the identity of the witch who had bewitched them. The girls both pointed their fingers directly at Tituba, the slave, as well as two other women, setting off the infamous Salem witch trials.

The first person to be hanged in Salem was Bridget Bishop, who had been married three times, ran two taverns, and dressed flamboyantly. At best, the reasons listed against her would not even stand a second thought in today's court of law, but it was enough back then to send her to the gallows. Most of those who were brought before the clergy were accused under "spectral evidence" – a testimony in which an individual claims that the accused harmed them in a dream or vision.

Because little to no evidence was required other than a spirit vision, testimonies flew left and right as villagers claimed to have been cursed by their neighbors or enemies. Pressures of a puritanical and patriarchal society, set the stage for repressed teenage girls to find themselves happily, and oddly, at the center of attention for the first and only time in their lives. Accusing your competition for a suitable husband became a convenient way to remove them as an obstacle.

Men, however, were not exempt from accusations and John Proctor was the first man to be executed in the trials due to his skepticism and doubts that witchcraft even existed.

While there has been much speculation on what led to the mania that became the Salem witch trials, ranging from psychological duress caused by living in such harsh environments, through to political social tensions, in 1976, Linda Caporal offered evidence that the trials had followed an outbreak of rye ergot and that the brief and intense illnesses suffered by so many of the townspeople were not bewitchment but rather the result of ergotism.

Ergot is the same psychoactive fungus that is suspected to have been used during the Greek Mysteries - an ancient festival that celebrated the magic of this world - and thrives in cold wet weather. Its effect is such that it can cause paranoia, hallucinations, spasms, cardiovascular issues, and stillborn babies. Its victims appear stoned and are prone to visions. The fungus is found in rye bread, and Caporal cited that in nearly all major areas where witch hunts had occurred globally, rye bread had been a staple of the diet at the time.

Despite these findings, and our new understanding of magic and witchcraft, the devil-worshiping smear campaign of the past still holds much stigma and fear.

In recent times, however, the word is being reclaimed by feminist movements and in Latin America, 'bruja' (witch) is used to denote a strong and capable female.

It's easy to dismiss the Salem trials as an irrational pitch-fork-wielding moment in history but the anxiety that gave way to the executions of innocent people is something that can still be observed these days with equally devastating consequences.

While the common person is no longer able to point fingers on the basis of spectral evidence and send someone to the gallows anymore, social media and computer screens have diminished responsibility, repercussions are low, and the result is a trigger-happy cancel-culture not too dissimilar to the medieval mob.

Our words still hold just as much power.

The witch was the product of an age of anxiety, and our fascination with this unruly magical worker reveals as much about our own fears and insecurities.

But as the saying goes: to point the finger at a witch is to admit to the existence of magic.

7

MIRRORS

I was lying face-up on a massage table with a white cotton blanket tucked around me.

My drug dealer's words were still bothering me, but I was trying to be in the present.

This time, I was attempting to cure myself with reiki.

"I don't know what's wrong with me, honestly," I had told my sister earlier that day, neglecting to tell her about the botched suicide. "I don't know if I can ever be normal again." I felt like a dingy lost at sea, whipped about through space and time. Untethered.

My sister explained her theory that I am the way I am because I am a spiky shape with lots of angles and edges.

"It's a good thing. Most people are like squares, you know. But you and I have all sorts of interesting corners, and that makes it, I guess, more of an interesting ride."

She paused to consider her words, "Besides, what's the fun of being a square!"

My sister is the kind of person who sends paper fortune tellers with little handwritten notes that say things like "Lord, give me chastity and continence – but not yet!" She has never been a square.

But these days, I envied squares. Spiky felt like more than I'd bargained for. I wished to be square. I'd even take a triangle.

I felt fragile to the point that I was now prone to bursting into tears at the most inappropriate and inconvenient moments – standing in the grocery line queue, paying for gas, walking the dog.

I smoked weed day in and out and just tried to block out the world as much as possible. My solution.

"I can relate," Sven, the reiki therapist, told me before the session. He was in his thirties, good-looking and from Germany, his accent thick but fluent.

"I was working as head of marketing for Audi in Berlin." He continued, "I had everything I thought I had ever wanted, but something wasn't right. I had a panic attack one day and decided to move to Bali, where I then learned reiki."

"How long until it all comes right?" I asked him, picking away at my cuticles.

"For me?" He pondered the question. "It took about a year before I truly trusted myself again. Everyone told me I was crazy. I had broken up with my partner, so there was a lot of loss happening."

He paused as his hands floated above my feet. "Tell you what, though, I wouldn't have changed anything. That was five years ago. Since then, I've met my husband, moved here, and set up my own studio. I'm happy probably for the first time in my life,"

His comment rattled me. I was trying to kill myself in every imaginable way. I wasn't sure I had a one-year runway.

As his hands hovered above my body wrapped up, I felt myself finally relax. The past week had been filled with the heaviness of suicidal thoughts followed by deep frustration and anger. My body was tired. All the stress and duress I had put myself through had worn me down. I didn't want to think about anything right now except his hands, somewhere over my legs. A touch that barely existed sent goosebumps running down my body.

He lightly pushed against the sides of my temples. I felt the mixed-up tension release, a surge of dopamine coursing through my body. Bliss! Human physical touch.

Transcending time, the past and the future merging into something so hilarious, I melted into the kaleidoscope of serotonin coursing through my veins.

"That wraps up the session, gorgeous lady." The words cut through my soul. I didn't want it to end. "There's some tea next to you. I'll give you some time to get up," he added and walked out, gently closing the door behind him, leaving me alone with the soft meditation sounds over the speaker and the air diffuser.

I felt fuzzy and struggled to frame myself back into my own reality. The delicious high from the reiki session was melting all the problems away. The vending machine had run out of coins, but I wasn't ready to face it all.

What if I asked him to hold his hands above my heart all day? What would he say? How much would that cost? I thought about asking but realized the futility. I couldn't afford that anymore, anyway.

As I sat up on the massage table, I came to face the wall across me with a giant round mirror I hadn't noticed when I first came in. It caught me off guard because there was no reflection, just a black surface looking back.

A dark obsidian of distorted nothingness.

It was designed to be this way, to reflect back nothingness.

I was gone. Erased.

I paused.

All this time, I had been plotting how to remove myself from the earth. Here it was, in this mirror. My wish was my command.

At first, this felt good.

After two years of loathing the reflection looking back at me, blackness was a respite.

The mirror cast a sheen of color as I pulled my sweater over my head, like the edge of an oil spill. It was so brief and fleeting that it made me pause for a moment, but just as quickly, it disappeared.

Only the room's soft lighting and vanilla-scented candles cast shadows of distorted outlines across its opaque surface.

The diffuser hummed away quietly in the background. The mist billowed up just under the mirror.

I shook my head and pulled my shoes back on. The candles were playing tricks on me.

Then, quite suddenly, it dawned on me.

Like a tub of warm water poured overhead, the penny dropped.

So clear and so obvious, there all along. It sent shivers down my spine. How had I missed it?

"*Everything going wrong in my life was a reflection of me.*" My drug dealer's words are clear as day.

A puzzle piece found behind the sofa.

A reflection of nothingness.

Just as I was.

It was all just a big mirror.

8

SOURCE CODE: MIRRORING

"Act, think, and feel like the version of yourself that already has the success you desire," my mentor had once instructed me.

He was my first business mentor and I had invested my last dollar in hiring him to help me turn around my failing business. I was pretty fresh to the business world and was struggling to keep it afloat, burning out in the process. A freelancer that thought it was cute to call herself an "agency" because I was so incredibly small. This investment was make-or-break. There was no Plan B. My little family and the home we had just built depended on it.

What a load of garbage is how I would have reacted to someone bringing up anything about mindset and mindfulness until I was in my thirties. To me, these ideas were wishful thinking, unfounded, and served no other purpose than a feel-good spiel.

But because I didn't have a Plan B, I took his advice, simple as that. I was in one of those universal financial pinches where your ass is literally pinned against a wall. You have no idea how you got there, but you're just praying you make it through in one piece. I had nothing to lose and everything to lose.

"Act, think, and behave like the version of yourself that already has the success you desire," my mentor had affirmed.

If I could embody the version of myself that I desired and bring forth this version of myself that acted like I had abundance and lots of money, then so it would be. The reflection of reality would mirror this back.

And so I would go and test drive dream cars. Shuffling my feet in tattered sneakers along the showrooms feeling like an imposter. I kept repeating the exercise until I felt at home. I did the same with multimillion-dollar oceanside houses.

And it worked really quickly. The business grew fast, with more revenues than I knew what to do with (twenty million dollars in three years). I landed the nice house, the nice car, and luxury business class seats. I achieved material success, and more.

It all worked so well that I was an immediate convert and advocate of meditation and mindfulness. I began to advise clients to incorporate it as part of running a business. I started to ship Muse meditation devices out to clients. In 2017, I even launched a course on mindfulness to share some of the techniques I had applied with success.

While *mirroring* sounds like something out of a sci-fi or far-fetched fantasy, it is rooted in the common-sense principle that the reality we experience is the direct result of past actions taken (or not taken) and our behaviors. These, in turn, are the result of the way we feel (emotions) which are regulated by perspectives and thought patterns.

Here's an example of how this phenomenon played out in my business with costly consequences. In 2018, I spent a small fortune producing a project I had prepared to launch to market.

It was called *Pay The F*cking Invoice* and was a reality series intended to help grow the reach and brand of an existing offer. I flew seven participants to New Zealand to work alongside me for seven weeks. The plan was to take them through a sort of freelancer turned agency bootcamp and record the whole thing.

The shooting itself had been so chaotic only because I didn't understand the rule of thumb of any film and documentary project (and any creation for that matter, including the magical sorts), which is that you must first know the intent. The day the cameraman arrived on the scene, he realized this had not been made clear. The project from there became an expensive and time-consuming affair requiring the review of hundreds of hours of footage just to spot the storylines for each episode.

Despite the madness, I was really proud of the project, and to be honest, at first, I truly believed it would be a one hit wonder, Netflix style. It was an entire production and kind of surreal to be a part of. And then something interesting happened.

You see, in my business career, I had never experienced a successful launch for myself, my own products, or offers. I had been part of and helped hundreds of successful client launches and was exposed almost daily to peers sharing wins from theirs, but mine always seemed to flop.

Most notably was the first business I had launched. It was called Yeity and was impossible to spell out on the phone. I had invested all my money into building a thirty-thousand-dollar app, and when it went live, it received only two subscribers (thanks, mom!).

My brain observed repetition in bad launches and then created a belief system to assist me in navigating my future circumstances.

All of my success had come from reiteration and optimization, never from one-hit wonder launches.

I wasn't aware of this at the time, of course. Beliefs are almost impossible to spot until after the fact (e.g., you don't always know you have limiting money beliefs until you find yourself with no money).

But I would often joke with my team and say things like, "I suck at launches," or "I've never had a good launch." It was a standing joke in the office (that and how I'm useless with remembering things and technology).

And because this belief existed within me, as we wrapped up editing and came closer to launch, my behaviors suddenly changed. It was subtle and not something I was perceptive to. For example, I would take forever to respond to the PR company I had hired to help me launch. It was a de-prioritized task. I never opened up more time slots in the sales team calendars as someone who would be anticipating a successful launch would.

The result: it was a failure of a launch, of course.

The whole irony of it all is that this experience, which was just a result of a perspective, further reinforced the original belief.

It became a self-perpetuating, self-enforcing cycle that was tricky to come out of, like a serpent with its tail in its mouth.

My thoughts directly shaped my actions and behaviors, which resulted in the abysmal launch, which then led to more bad thoughts, which fed the next cycle.

Mirroring.

Throughout this process, the language I used and the words that came out of my mouth were a big clue as to what I was actually enchanting for myself, though I was not perceptive to it enough at the time.

The dysfunction and depression that were happening in my life were no different. It was the output of my own input. I was so fixated and focused on solving and fixing the problems that I failed to notice that in doing so I was feeding myself more problems.

9

SOURCE CODE: PERSPECTIVE

"The only things we perceive are our perceptions."

— GEORGE BERKELEY

A delightful tale that perfectly encapsulates the power of perspective that I first heard told through the late quantum psychologist Robert Anton Wilson in *Quantum Psychology* is about an old farmer who one day loses his coin purse.[1] Searching everywhere, the farmer becomes convinced that his neighbor's young son has stolen it. The following day, the farmer bumps into the boy who casts furtive and suspicious glances and this enrages the farmer. He decides he will storm over to his neighbor's house and demand the boy return his coin purse.

As the farmer is about to knock on the door, his wife calls out, "Dear, I found your purse. It was behind the sofa!"

The story is told by Taoist philosophers to contemplate the following: Was the boy acting guilty because the farmer believed he was guilty and so, therefore, the farmer saw guilt in the boy? Or was the boy acting guilty because the farmer's own aggressive behavior towards him brought out the behavior?

Either way, it's clear that the farmer's perspective shaped his very experience. And on some level, we can all relate to this story – seeing things that simply aren't there or misreading situations with embarrassing consequences.

Our perspectives structure our reality, and this is risky simply because of how perspectives are formulated in the first place.

Every moment of every second, billions of information signals bombard our nervous system. In *Molecules of Emotion*, Dr. Candace B. Pert explains, "The nervous system is not capable of taking in everything [sensory information], but can only scan the outer world for material that it is prepared to find by virtue of its wiring hookups."[2]

Our five senses – sight, sound, touch, smell, and taste – do their best to create what we perceive as our physical reality by deciphering a small fraction of the information being received. Still, even then, there is too much coming in at any given moment, and so, we run pattern recognition scripts to draw on past experiences and observations to extrapolate future scenarios.

The midbrain, which filters every sensory experience through the lens of bias, even controls the direction of the eyeball and what is allowed to pass through the retinas.

All this complex algorithm of sifting and sorting leads to a perception. A map formulated to help us navigate our way, or as the late Robert Anton Wilson would say, a *reality tunnel.*

World-renowned neuroscientist, Professor Ramachandran, explains that the brain is both a storyteller and a fact-checker. The storyteller is responsible for making up constant theories of the world, which helps us to conserve energy when it comes to decision-making. Such is the power of the brain at filling in the vacuum of information that it can cause perceptual illusions, such as patients hallucinating comic book scenes, or even physical sensations - such as a man who once claimed to have orgasms in his amputated foot when he had sexual intercourse.[3]

A simple exercise to illustrate this, Ramachandran shares, is to place your hand under a table and then to have someone else stroke your hand as well as the surface of the table simultaneously. After a while the brain will blend in the experience and you will begin to feel the strokes on the surface of the table. The brain essentially merges in with the table – illustrating how arbitrary and malleable perceptions really are. And so, even though we like to think our models of reality are foolproof and accurate, they are always full of holes by their very nature because we construct them in the first place.

We are pattern recognition machines that find meaning through the mess of it all. And when we successfully detect a pattern, it stimulates our reward centers.

In this way, patterns are habit-forming and we fail to notice the hundreds or thousands of pieces of information that aren't repeated or the red flags right under our noses simply because they do not conform to existing dogmas or beliefs.

This mechanic of reality is not dissimilar to how the Facebook newsfeed works. A complex algorithm that tracks what you engage in, which sites you visit, and what triggers you, and on the other side, a mirror of the initial input pops out.

The newsfeed of reality is the same.

Where we give our focus is how we ultimately shape our perception of reality. And our perception of reality is ultimately what determines our experience of it.

Our lives are filled with examples of how this shows up. For instance, when we believe we are undeserving, we don't ask for pay raises. We settle for rejection. We don't walk away from dysfunctional relationships. We don't take risks. We stay at a level that keeps confirming we aren't worthy. We are the ones that keep ourselves there.

When we believe everyone is a cheater or out to get us. We accuse easily and have less empathy. We tend to be involved in more litigation. We experience betrayals because we are the first ones to lawyer up. Ironically, this all leads to the very thing we resisted or feared to begin with.

Skewed perception can also cause us to walk away from perfectly good relationships because we cannot accept that they won't blow up somehow in our faces or that we are deserving.

But a newsfeed is never the truth of how the world really is. It is merely the truth of how one nervous system has prescribed meaning from the patterns it has observed.

Science is only just now really beginning to understand how the algorithm of the mind appears to construe a subjective physical experience and the picture-taking shape is that the perceiver is the one who determines if it is a wave or a particle.

Perception is relative – a dual to another point of view. The magician should, therefore, always question their own perspective and discard any attempt to prove "right" and "wrong", understanding full well that the answer will depend on who's asking.

As a mentor and friend Jesse Elder once told me, "It's not about 'is it true or false' but rather 'is it useful to me?'" "

My perception of my reality was that I was a failure because I had lost the material success I had gained. This belief was neither true nor false but certainly it was not very useful to my life experience as it made me entertain suicidal thoughts.

This "is it useful" rule of thumb extends to magic itself – regardless of what perceptions you may have about it, ask yourself if it serves you to believe what you believe in.

Is magic real? Maybe, maybe not. Is it more useful to believe that you have dominion and creative capacities over your own reality vs not? Most definitely.

And ultimately, whatever you believe is what you will be mirrored back to you.

Ritual – Creating a Talisman

A talisman, otherwise known as an effigy or lamp, is a "magical device" that is charged with a specific intent or purpose and then worn or hidden somewhere to create the magical effect. This type of magic has been pervasive in Indian religious traditions since the time of the Atharva Veda.

In Tibetan magic, the stages of crafting a talisman are broken down into "sngags" (recitation), "las" (action), and "thun" (material or substance).[4]

It is helpful to create your own talisman with the intent of *remembering* magic. A physical object that helps you to perceive the octarine is the magician's color as shared in Terry Pratchett's *The Color of Magic*, both in yourself and in all other things.

A talisman can take almost any object or form, from a crystal to a stick. I own a moonstone crystal that reminds me of the octarine color.

To create yours collect materials from nature or objects that appeal to you and combine them together to craft an effigy of sorts.

When I first attempted this, I found a twig that stuck out to me and long blades of cutty grass. I wrapped the grass around the stick and cushioned it with moss.

As you craft your talisman, recite the intention or incantation, or visualize and feel the end result. Place the sensation of remembering magic, of trusting the forces that play between the physical and nonphysical.

Once you have created your talisman, place it somewhere where you will only encounter it every so often (a few times per week). While it can be helpful to intentionally remind yourself of your inner magic every time you see your talisman, this won't be required as you would have planted the intent subconsciously, and seeing it will be enough to stir up the remembering, even if only subconsciously.

10

SEX SWINGS & MAGIC

I'm going to bend you over and fuck you till you confess how you've been a dirty little slut.

My ex didn't love me anymore, but he still wanted to fuck.

The territory was slippery, this much I was certain of.

He felt like the platform that had existed before the monster had made itself known in my life, something sturdy to reach for like a buoy in a storm, connected to parts of myself before I had lost my mind. Perhaps he was the key to finding these parts again?

I lay on my bed, touching myself. I didn't care what had been said or done. All would be forgiven. I was lonely, so terribly lonely.

Come over, I begged him in a text message. *Show me.*

I would have given myself to him instantly if he'd asked.

I'll come visit you tomorrow after I finish my shift, he promised.

I'm a sucker for circuits of punishment.

That day, giddy and full of fantasy, I went to the sex shop to purchase a sex swing. Just after I paid for it and got back in the car, he messaged me a long text. In short: *I'm confused. I'm so sorry.* He ended the text by letting me know he doesn't think meeting me is a good idea. Good bye.

I looked over at the $200 sex swing in the passenger seat and a hot flush of embarrassment passed through me. I wanted to melt and cry and dig myself into a hole and die.

The failed suicide attempt was a few weeks behind me and there'd been no more since then, thankfully, but it hadn't been easy.

Understanding it was all a reflection was one thing. At first, it made me feel empowered, like Indiana Jones holding the golden scarab. I had solved the puzzle! I understood I needed to simply change how I felt, and the reflection would change. *Knowing* this was inherently different from doing it. I had become more proactive and intentional with my daily meditations but still, I felt raw from the heartbreak.

And so I set the intention to prove to myself that magic existed once more. I told myself, "*If this life is supposed to feel easy and well for me, show me proof that I am deserving.*"

And strange, unexpected little things began to show up around me. So subtle they could have been easily brushed off as coincidence.

For instance – I walked to the beach on a blustery day not long after having set the intention to be shown this magic only to discover twenty conch shells (large sea snails) on the sand and seagulls circling above. Most of the shells had been picked clean, which I kept as a keepsake, and the remainder I threw back in the ocean. Not long after this, a friend offered her family home to me located right on the water. A blissful and serene place where I would listen to the lapping of the waves against the decking. Solutions were springing up.

In and of themselves and singularly, these serendipitous moments weren't enough to swing me back into the land of the living, but their meaning began to compound and was being received. I was being shown.

It felt like a nudge, like I, the universe, or source, was helping me refocus back to life's benevolence.

I turned to nature to become more perceptive to it, to heal.

I cut twigs from trees in the yard and propagated them, watching them grow roots like little white dog hairs in their vases. I felt a sensation of flow and easiness when I dug my fingernails into the earth or watched a new leaf unfurl on a seedling.

The flutter of a butterfly wing, the prism of a rainbow, the double helix of a coil of DNA imagined in the pupil of an eye, and the sun reflecting off a spider's web.

Octarine.

The color of magic is a non-color. An evanescence of blueish-green and pink-purples.

It requires intentional perception to see it.

I couldn't see it in myself yet, but it was easy to spot when I looked up into the night sky or at the velvety pink bulbs of the magnolia tree. I couldn't see heaven from my vantage point, but when I looked up under the cape of the toadstool mushroom, I saw the architecture of the Gods.

11

GUIDANCE

I've been so young for so long and so old for longer – so heart-wrinkled and naive all at once. So brow-furrowed but heart-open, too; a detective. Snooping yet easily sidetracked. I'll believe anything because I want to understand, yet understanding can sometimes organize itself like a series of false starts.

— DURGA CHEW-BOSE, *TOO MUCH AND NOT THE MOOD*

Since time immemorial, humans have sought to divine answers from the nonphysical using all sorts of tools and techniques. Rune stones, tea leaves, tarots, and anything with symbolic meaning have been used in some shape or form to access information from the invisible.

Sycomancy, for example, is an ancient form of botanomancy: the use of plants to divine. Using the leaves of a fig tree or sycamore, the diviner writes down answers across the leaves. The slower they dry, the more favorable the answer.

During Plato's time, divination was accomplished through theurgy – the evocation of spirits – and oracles and theurgists were considered to be the key mediums through which contact with the gods could be made. Guidance sought included the provision of ritual instruction, practical advice, metaphysical and cosmological instruction and tools for contemplation and meditation.

Second sight and clairvoyance can also be established through dreams, and books are one of my personal favorite ways to divine. Setting an intention and then opening up a page at random often yields shockingly accurate results.

So long as meaning can be ascribed, there are no rules or limits to what can be used as methods of divination.

I've even had a witchy friend confess to me that she uses her toes to determine guidance!

And while studies show that divination is a veritable phenomenon, the real question remains: is fate fated, or are psychics picking up on an information field of probabilities or – better yet – enchanting the future itself?

For example, I once did a tarot reading for a friend that said she would have a career change. She brushed it off, stating she was happy with where she was at, but five months later, she quit her job and found a better one. Did the prediction come true because it was fate or because she enchanted herself into that version of reality?

If beliefs and perceptions structure reality, then the risk with divination is that we can ultimately prophesize our worlds through the act of divining.

This is why Peter Carroll warns in *Liber Kaos* to "divine short, enchant long!".

Personally, I see divination as a process of communication with intuition/creative core/self. A way to tap into and access patterned information all around.

That you can always shift directions and make something wrong right or vice versa – and that there are no fixed fates. Rather, the creative process is to figure out which probabilities and fates hold the highest version of ourselves and to move ourselves in this direction.

Again, I choose to believe this not because it has necessarily been proven true in a lab, but because it is more useful to believe that – even when I make wrong choices – all can be righted, and doors will still open.

While divining, it's helpful to avoid ego-based or closed-ended questions and to keep intentions or questions open-ended.

For example, avoid things like, "Will Tim text me back?" or "Will this client say 'yes' or 'no'?" because these questions are ego-based. The creative core does not inherently care about "Tim" or a particular client, nor does it care about money.

Instead, keep to open-ended questions that are more along the lines of, "What is the path?" or, "What should I do?" or, "Where should I go?"

Guidance can also take the form of what I call "signs of alignment". A sign of alignment is an area in our lives that shows growth, love, and expansion without much effort or exertion on our part.

For example, this could include an email list that grows quietly in the background, people reaching out about a particular offer or service, a friendly offer of help, or random coincidences or opportunities that present themselves.

Activities, places, creations, hobbies, people, and experiences can also show signs of alignment based on whether they naturally place us in better feeling states.

There are always signs of alignment around. If you do not believe this statement, if it feels that everything is going wrong or bad, it is simply because you are not perceptive enough (focused too much on the lack/gap or problems).

If this is the case, set the intention that the signs will become more apparent and obvious to you.

The theme of magic itself presented itself in my life as aligned guidance. At the time, I was working with private clients on business growth but encountering resistance – both trying to grow the business as well as mentally. However, I had just launched my podcast The Flow Protocols and it was steadily growing without any ads or effort.

Accordingly, I re-prioritized my time and shifted focus to the podcast episodes, going deeper into topics of magic. Instead of getting stuck into a three-year tailspin of depression again, I was able to guide myself back into a good head space within a matter of days by simply following the guidance coming through.

Mind you, this guidance didn't make much sense at the time. Some financial complications meant I needed a new income stream and should have been focusing on income-generating activities. The podcast was not making money, and the writing itself would not be the fast money solution I needed at that time either.

And yet, as I went into these activities, my emotional tension softened and the strangest of things happened. It also allowed me to see that the structure I was moving toward before – though I pushed for it and thought I really wanted it – was actually not aligned, and that the resistance was there to break me down just enough to allow the shift in perspective to occur.

Alignment can show up in the most obscure ways, so you need to keep your mind and eyes open for it.

For example, I worked with one entrepreneur who deeply desired to get involved in creating a charitable foundation but had always prevented herself from doing so because she felt she didn't quite have the capital and wasn't there financially to do such a thing. She was encountering all sorts of resistance in her digital marketing agency – clients ditching and having to look for jobs. At an event she attended, she met a person with a legal background who offered her free assistance in launching her new idea. This was a sign of alignment for her. Again, this doesn't necessarily mean the lawyer is the answer or solution, but this was a thread of guidance compelling her focus, a solution being presented without effort.

By simply placing our attention and intent on receiving more support where the alignment exists, we can more easily allow ourselves to create and play in the space we desire.

Below, I list some of my favorite methods of divination. As a rule of thumb, you'll want to avoid divination work while you are in a "bad" mood or not feeling well as typically this will only result in doom and gloom answers.

Grimoire

For as long as I can remember, I have kept a journal. One of my favorite things about this activity is that, often, when I need guidance to overcome an obstacle or moment of disorder in my life, I will open up a page of an old journal and get to read advice from myself from another time and place. Reading older entries often helps me remember how I had encountered many moments of chaos and unknowns before and always overcame them. It helps me to stay in my power. It is also beneficial to keep a grimoire of your conjurings and rituals so you can review it at least once or twice a year. A grimoire is basically a journal or written record of your magical attempts. Doing this will allow you to see what spells and rituals worked, which will help you refine and better understand what techniques work best for you. From there, your magic will become more and more potent and optimized.

Books

I have been using this method for some time and it is a personal favorite.

Again, set the intention or identify your question if you have one. Transfer the energy of the intention to the book, and then randomly open up a page. What is being said on the page? What resonates and sticks out to you? This is the message your own guidance wishes you to know. Whatever meaning you ascribe to it is the correct interpretation.

When I asked a group of practicing alchemists to try this exercise, one person in the group was encountering tension with a friend that had betrayed her. She had been feeling anger and bitterness over the situation. When she opened the book it was immediately a chapter and a passage on letting go of animosity towards others.

Some people might be shocked to know I have made important and significant life decisions based on divination from books.

Tarot

Tarot is another tool I have become familiar with and often use as a way to guide myself.

It is usually recommended that you try to familiarize yourself with the cards and their meanings before you do a reading. To "transfer" your energy to the cards, some practitioners even recommend placing the cards under your pillow for a night or two.

I use tarots either to help me find clarity of guidance when a crossroads or dysfunction presents itself, or I use them as a general way to communicate to myself by diving in with an open heart to whatever comes through.

Again, we should avoid pulling cards when we are not feeling well.

Scrying

Scrying is a technique whereby a reflective surface (usually a black obsidian, crystal, or bowl filled with water) is stared into to expand perception. This is one of the oldest techniques of magic, but will require some practice on your part.

As you stare into the surface, allow images to come without focusing too intently. You'll want to do this in a dimly lit room with no lights above to reflect on the surface. Candles are good for this exercise.

This technique can be especially useful if you struggle to perceive visuals with closed eyes and it will help develop your intuition and psychic abilities. Write down whatever symbols come through. Your immediate gut reaction to how you interpret the symbols is their true meaning. Once the rational mind starts to dissect the meaning of symbols, it's no longer true intuition.

Practice this regularly for best results. Again, stay away if you are not feeling good (hungry, tired, stressed, upset, etc.)

12

TAPROOTS

In its full maturity, the monstera plant, not unlike the one in my living room, can reach heights of up to 60 feet, with huge fenestrations. It does this by attaching itself and climbing up a host tree.

But unlike a parasite that uses and abuses hospitality, the monstera only uses its host as support and does not kill it. The two plants coexist in harmony.

The fruit of the monstera plant looks like an oddly-shaped pinecone or a corn on the cob – much like the tattoo on my left arm. A monstrosity of a thing that had seemed like a good idea at the time, as these things often go. I had it done on the back of a seven day meditation retreat before the monster had entered my life.

Two thousand souls desperate to find answers, themselves, or material gain in the coffers of spirituality. We would rise at five am and spend six hours meditating under the guru's guidance. My legs would ache and – try as I might to maintain a straight posture – I was all but hunch-backed by the end of the day.

The point of all the meditation – we were informed – was to enter altered states of consciousness by triggering our pineal gland. A tiny pine cone-looking organ residing inside of the human brain and said to be connected to the source codes of life itself.

"Did you know that when you drown, the pineal gland releases DMT? It's supposed to make death a pleasant experience," one of the attendees had excitedly told me.

And so, we eagerly sucked air in through our mouths and took ourselves to the brink of meditative exhaustion in a bid to experience otherworldly euphoria.

And it worked for many. I would watch comrades fall to the floor from their chairs in spasms of orgasmic bliss. Moaning and groaning as if the gods themselves were rubbing them off.

While I suspected many of them were faking the experience itself, I desperately wanted what they were having, to trigger this little gland that looked like a pinecone. So I would take deep intentional breaths and hold them to the point of dizziness all the while thinking:

Tickle, tickle, goddammit.

But enlightenment was not to be mine on this trip, not in that way anyways. This didn't stop me from feeling a slight sense of spiritual superiority from all the meditation, and when I returned to the city from the conference, I smoked a big joint and decided I would have this gland tattooed on my arm.

The same arm I had earmarked for a full sleeve design for years. I had the whole design planned out, there would be a wolf howling at a moon and a swirl of a galaxy behind it. I had told myself that when the business had cracked the million-dollar mark, I would treat myself to the sleeve. I even had the tattoo artist I wanted already lined up.

But there's a saying that goes something like "If you want to make God laugh just tell him your plans," and just like that, all my tattoo dreams were thrown out the window when I got high and instead put a great big pine cone on the real estate that was reserved for my sleeve.

The wolf and galaxy were abandoned, with much chagrin, for a garden, where I tried to blend in the protruding ugliness of the pinecone with roses and bees.

It bothered me greatly for the first year, I had even gone to see a skin clinic and paid for one tattoo removal session. But abandoned the quest of erasing it partly due to the pain of the removal process and partly because the grotesque corn on the cob-looking cone eventually started to grow on me. It was like a reckless part of myself had left a mark on me, to let me know she was still there.

What most people don't realize about the monstera plant, with its big cheese-hold-looking leaves, is that it possesses superpowers.

If it's left in the dark, the plant will exhibit negative phototropism, where new leaves will grow towards the dark rather than the light. In the jungle, darkness signals the presence of a larger tree that monstera can climb up to reach sunlight. Darkness signals a host.

Padding out the jungle floor with fat aerial roots that resemble thin pale limbs reaching out for a tree to latch onto, the plant hooks on and begins its ascent.

The entropy of darkness creates the order of growth.

In this way, I had also come to find myself in the dark, my own aerial roots tapping around the blackness, hoping to land on the trunk of something solid I could rely on.

Everytime I tapped around I found no one but myself, my own reflection staring back in the mirror. I forced myself to acknowledge the woman staring back, to see if I could find myself behind the mess, and slowly something new began to appear. Octarine in my own eyes. Barely imperceptible, but there nevertheless.

I continued to pad out around myself and the more I did, the more I came back unscathed, and the more my confidence grew. The more I dared to venture deeper, to stare for longer.

Tap, tap, tap, went my roots.

Gradually, the shadows of the night that had tormented me before shapeshifted into the foundations from which I could see myself once more.

In the undertow, looking up at the mature monstera above, it's easy to feel like something has gone amiss, that things aren't adding up.

But it's in the undertow that the rot of the humus giving off steam in the misty morning serves as sustenance to the precarious balance of life.

It's in the undertow that beastly mutations take place. Transformations of the grotesque sort.

And it was in the undertow that the part of myself that had been trapped and lost for so long got absorbed into another part of myself.

My own taproots came across something soft. A warm pulse.

My own hand. Softly guiding, softly warming.

It was the undertow that taught me that it was nature that invented blackness.

13

INTENT

"For I am I: ergo, the truth of myself; my own sphinx, conflict, chaos, vortex – asymmetric to all rhythms, oblique to all paths. I am the prism between black and white: my own unison in duality."

— *AUSTIN OSMAN SPARE*

If language *is the* highest form of symbolism and enchantment to humans, then it is a fair statement to say that if one does not know how to properly communicate their intention – either verbally or written – then they probably do not understand it themselves well enough to eventuate it.

For this reason, intention sits at the core of a magical practice. Without it, much like my pet production *Pay the Invoice* project, we end up with disorder and chaos.

At face value, answering the question, "What do you want?" seems simple enough. Most of us will immediately think of the big home, loving relationships and lots of money. And this is usually where the wheels also start to come undone.

I had spent my whole life aspiring for the riches only to discover that fulfillment, joy, and peace of mind are not conditional. Meaning that they are never acquired through outside things.

Ultimately the creative core – the part of ourselves that crafts from the invisible – doesn't really care about things or experiences. What it truly desires is a state of being. A feeling.

I didn't really care about the fancy office, the big team, the industry recognition, or the followers. I wanted those things because they made me *feel* important. They made me *feel* respect and pride.

I wanted the travel because I wanted to *feel* extroversion, adventure, and affluence. I wanted a nice car because I wanted to *feel* a sense of accomplishment.

The creative core only truly desires feelings.

And when we ignore this and chase the things we think will make us feel a certain way about ourselves or life, we create conditions over our intent and thereby invite chaos. We become trapped by those things acquired. We create more resistance to help us remember that we are alchemists, always capable of delivering exactly what we seek – unconditionally.

When we can get really clear on what state we desire – our true uncorrupted will (at that moment in time) – we can craft it into our very realities by practicing well-being within ourselves first.

Love, peace of mind, confidence, fulfillment, purpose, affluence, respect, freedom, vitality, and connection. These are the things we ultimately seek.

If we require a specific thing to bring these states to us, we should first be asking ourselves why this is. The most fun and joy in life is discovering how to find this state without needing those things. Trusting fully that once we teach ourselves this first, reality has no choice but to come play ball. More circumstances, experiences, resources, and relationships that align with what it is we desire will come to us as and when we need them. Mirroring.

And so, this brings us to the intent of magic. Instead of trying to use magic to gain specific things, such as a particular job, car, or house, or to make our neighbors nicer, which magic can most definitely also help with, we should instead bypass the middleman and go straight to the treasure pot and ensure we serve ourselves at the highest level.

Of course, the question then becomes, what is the state you desire? Sure, at a high level, we all desire love, peace of mind, confidence, and fulfillment, but this leaves us with too wide a net to cast.

Likewise, this question isn't always easy to answer, only because our own thoughts can be difficult to decipher. The ego is easy to muddle with the creative core if we are only paying attention to thought patterns.

This is where the principle of mirroring, as shared in the Kybalion,[1] comes into service:

Everything is dual; everything has poles; everything has its pair of opposites; like and unlike are the same; opposites are identical in nature, but different in degree; extremes meet; all truths are but half-truths; all paradoxes may be reconciled.

Not only does reality mirror us, but so too do emotions mirror each other. Meaning that emotional states all have an equal and opposite dual.

Love is the same but a polar of depression. Because when you feel hopeless, worthless, and empty, you cannot be more disconnected from the sensation of love.

Overwhelm is the same but dual of flow. Because when you are in flow, you can work twelve hours and keep going, but when you are overwhelmed, two hours of work feels like a brick truck.

Anxiety and fear are the same but opposites of play and courage. Because when you are in a state of courage and play, you are resilient to fear. You can bungee jump off a bridge and override strong biological fear triggers with little effort.

Anger and frustration are the same but duals of empathy and peace of mind. When you are frustrated with your progress, it is because you do not feel secure with where you are.

When we feel jealous, we are being instructed to transmute inspiration. And if we can change our perspective to feel inspired instead of jealous, our world will transform in ways we could not have even scripted for ourselves, in a way that benefits all those around us.

And so emotions communicate to us, through the principle of duality, what it is that our creative core really wants.

When we are afraid, we desire courage and play.

When we are lonely, we desire company.

When we are confused, we desire clarity.

And on and on.

Understanding this mechanism of polarity helps us to set the compass of intention.

It gives us the recipe we now need to work with. A big red arrow pointing exactly to what we seek and desire, telling us "Learn to give yourself *this* state, unconditionally, and you will expand beyond your wildest dreams."

The Intent of Magic

Based on your own emotional guidance system and the principle of duality, what have you identified as the true desire of your creative core?

What state of being is it that you seek that you are being asked to transmute? What conditions in your existing reality stop you from having this? What conditions have you created around your creative core's true will?

Here's a rough overview of the polarity principle of emotions to help you better understand what your true will desires you to craft for yourself:

Boredom → Inspiration/Enthusiasm

Confusion → Clarity

Trapped/Stuck → Secure

Jealous → Inspired

Angry → Empathetic

Insecure → Confident

Anxious/Afraid → Courageous/Playful

Overwhelmed → Flow

Depressed/Hopeless → Grateful/Love

Unconditional Love

"Till death do us part" are words taken seriously by many. A vow to love our partners unconditionally, through thick and thin, even if they grow hairs on their chin.

We extend this kind of unconditional love to our children. Our kid, for example, could have murdered someone, and despite this we would still, somehow, find love for them.

And although we grasp the concept of unconditional love and know how to give and receive it from others, we do not hold the same standard when it comes to ourselves.

When it comes to ourselves, the rules change.

The relationship that we have with ourselves and our own well-being *is* conditional.

I will only feel financially free when I make the money...

I will only feel worthy and loved when I have a loving partner...

I will only feel purposeful when I have something to strive for…

I will only feel chilled out and forgiving when that idiot stops being an idiot…

When, when, when.

But if reality is a mirror, a reflection of the outcome of past actions and perspectives, how could it ever validate and make the first move in such a way? Conditions never work.

The reflection can only change when that which is reflected alters. Once we understand what our true will is and what we really desire, we must first learn to give it to ourselves before we can expect it to show up in our lives.

And so, the first task of the alchemist is to be willing to give themselves the state of being they ultimately desire *before* reality corroborates.

14

SOURCE CODE: RED/GREEN

"I dunno Cat. The whole exercise just made me feel even more anxious." Those were the words of my client. I had started to take on private coaching clients again, helping to mentor them through business challenges. It was light work. I was still feeling raw from the previous two years and wasn't yet ready for a full workload but by the same token, I found deep purpose and flow in supporting others and was being called to show up as a mentor once more.

My client was an entrepreneur in his mid-thirties who had suffered some traumas in his past. He was in an employment role that felt out of place and wanted the confidence to break away and start his own business again. The last time he'd attempted such a task, he'd grown a successful agency but it had all come crashing down when personal reasons had led him to close it all down. A story I could relate to.

I tasked him with techniques I had myself used when growing my business – simple things at first like vision boards and writing letters to his past self, but something wasn't adding up.

I couldn't place my finger on it, but I observed that while some of my clients seemed to benefit from these exercises, for others it only aggravated their fears or frustration.

Was it their history? I asked myself one day while gardening. I mentally combed through their timelines and I realized this was not the variable. Some of those who succeeded with the tasks had even more harrowing pasts than those who hadn't.

Was it their intelligence? Again, I followed the maze and came to a dead end, this was not it either.

As I continued to unravel the thread, the variable suddenly made itself clear and known to me. It was their emotional state.

When a client was attempting affirmations when they felt "bad", this seemed to make things worse. On the flipside, when the same task was attempted from a "feel good" state, suddenly, the results skyrocketed.

Emotions were the deciding factor.

And so was born the red light/green light system.

To better explain how this works it is first important to understand what exactly emotions are and how they come to shape our realities.

The Islamic scholar Ya qūb ibn Isḥāq al-Kindī, whose work was highly influential in Western magic and esotericism, postulated that everything which actually exists in the world sends out rays. Vibrations. These rays fill the entire world of the elements in their own way and the human body, just like any other physical mass, receives and emits information, which is regulated by our emotions.

Emotions are chemical responses to our perceptions of our reality. They occur when neurotransmitters make electrical leaps across brain synapses when information is received. This information is then carried off through the vast and complex network of the body's receptors.[1] The result is biochemicals flushing through our system, changing the very makeup of our well-being.

We receive information through our five senses, which then allow us to craft perceptions from which we navigate through our lives.

What we perceive to be reality is merely a construct of this sensory transcription and – as we now understand – our perceptions should always be questioned.

But if our eyes, touch, smell, and ears cannot be fully trusted, then how can we possibly hope to navigate our way?

Cue: emotions.

They are the guidance system that tells us exactly how to stay the course to our own alignment, our own space of effortless co-creation.

Innate technology that enables us to take advantage of the resonance existing between all things to navigate both physical and nonphysical dimensions.

This navigational system is connected to parts of the energetic world that the rational mind cannot access (as the brain bases decisions simply on past experiences and observations filtered through pattern recognition software). It knows that Byron, who will make your coffee, is the key to planting the seed of an idea and that you had to miss the bus in order to find yourself in that coffee shop to encounter him. It understands correspondences that exist in an infinite world of probabilities that the rational mind simply could never connect.

And while the idea that a biological being could transcribe rays or vibrations may sound ludicrous, it is the standard.

For example, birds navigate across the world by tuning into the earth's magnetic field. Snakes find their way around using infrared radiation.

But here's where things get tricky.

Most of us go about experiencing emotions as the result of our physical reality. Something someone says or does, what our bank accounts look like, our relationship statuses, etc., determines how we feel.

As Dr. Joe Dispenza explains in his book *Breaking the Habit of Being Yourself*:[2]

By definition, emotions are the end products of past experiences in life. When you're in the midst of an experience, the brain receives vital information from the external environment through five different sensory pathways (sight, smell, sound, taste, and touch). As that cumulative sensory data reaches the brain and is processed, networks of neurons arrange themselves into specific patterns reflecting the external event. The moment those nerve cells string into place, the brain releases chemicals. Those chemicals are called "emotions" or "feelings."

We take the construct of reality formulated through our senses as truth and do not realize that we are able to guide ourselves beyond perceptual cues.

For the longest time, I believed my emotions were part of the human condition, that I was cursed with them, and that I would be better off without them. Emotions, however, play a critical role in our circumstances. A study conducted on patients with brain tumors who had the parts of their brain where emotions are created lobotomized showed that without emotions,[3] we would not be capable of making even the most straightforward decisions, like picking what cereal to eat. Emotions – the way you feel – are responsible for all the decisions and behaviors you take. They are an essential part of your toolbox used to craft reality.

And because they determine all our actions and choices, they shape our reality.

But it gets better. Not only are emotions a biochemical byproduct of perspectives and thoughts (synaptic firing) that serve to attract and repulse things to us, they communicate to us information beyond sight, sound, smell, touch, and taste.

They are our own high-technology navigational system that allows us to steer through the wavelength reality of information all around us. They understand precisely how to fulfill what we desire using the path of least resistance because they are the vibrational output system of our physical vessel. They are connected to our true, uncorrupted will.

They are superior to your logical and rational mind because they have access to higher-quality information than your five sensory receptors do. They are superior to the rational mind because they communicate to you EXACTLY what you really believe or perceive because all emotions are the result of synaptic connections in the brain (thoughts), and while it is almost impossible for you to try to guess what you really believe in or call out your own perspectives (because we've already established, perspectives are tunnel vision), emotions tell it to you straight up. They tell you what you really perceive at that moment, what you really believe.

In the world of tech, it is often said that the best technology is always the simplest, the one with the cleanest and easiest UX – something even a five-year-old could grasp. And in this way, emotions have to represent the highest form of technology because the navigational system you are in possession of is very simple.

When you feel "bad", you are telling yourself STOP.

"Bad-feeling" emotions let you know you are off course and "good-feeling" emotions – on the other hand – tell you when you are on course. Simple.

Red/green.

Bad-feeling emotions are called "red light" and are those that stress the parasympathetic nervous system. They include apathy, depression, anxiety, fear, boredom, anger, frustration, unfulfillment, stress, tiredness, hunger, and many more. While there are thousands of "bad-feeling" emotions, they are all easily identifiable by how they feel in the body.

Stress, for example, feels bad because it literally stresses the nervous system. It lowers serotonin, slows digestion and gives you wrinkles.

While there is a huge range of feelings and states – as numerous as there are shades of colors – from apathetic through to pure joy and love, it is very obvious which feels good and which feels bad to you.

Keep in mind, though, that while I termed them "bad feeling" emotions, they are not inherently evil or something we should aspire to eliminate altogether. Emotions are a communication signal so the goal is not to never experience a red light emotion again or villainize them. That would be the equivalent of taking up a vendetta against your home's wi-fi router. Red light emotions are crucial for expansion and transformation as they communicate true desires. Without this, it would only be a homogeneous substance of love that could not allow for the expansion of life or creative expression.

Red light emotions feel bad because they communicate that your own perspective, the synaptic connections being made in your brain, are no longer fulfilling your true will. In other words, whatever you are thinking at that moment is incorrect. It is an invitation to flip perspectives.

Red light, as in, come to a complete stop, do not pass. Do not want to make important decisions, don't hire, don't fire, don't invest, don't start the project, don't email, don't bother with the sales call, don't text back. Red = stop. This explains the phenomena I observed with my clients and the differing results they experienced.

This also applies to magic. If you attempt rituals, conjurings, or visualization exercises in a red light state, you will likely create more chaos for yourself.

Instead, the priority should be to get back into green.

Green light emotions are any emotional state that feels good in the body. This could include peace of mind, playfulness, excitement, confidence, play, love, and gratitude. Again, while there is an entire spectrum of emotions, green light emotions are easy to recognize because they don't cause tension in our bodies. They feel good to us. Instead of stressing our parasympathetic system, they actually strengthen it; they boost immunity.

When we are in green light states, we will observe a lightness of being in the body, which will result in more of the same likeness reflected back to us. These emotions feel good because they signal that we match the perspective to our own path of least resistance, that we are rooted to our creative core.

Green light means GO. When you are in green, you can push the pedal, make the investment, hire/fire, say yes, respond to the text, send the email, take the sales call, or quit the job.

This also means "Go" with magic and conjurings. A green light emotion tells you that you are locked into your creative core; now is the time to craft your perfect reality. Visualize specific intentions, journal them, and invoke them within yourself.

Here's an example of how red light/green light recently played out for me in my own life.

Late one night, I opened up the Facebook app on my phone and immediately saw a snarky comment left on one of my posts. My blood was boiling because I felt the person was basically discrediting my work. What's more, this person had been a recent client.

As my heart began beating louder in my head, I felt the sound in the room dull. I was so angry. I had given this client everything and they had done well.

"Who are they to say this to me?" I said to myself out loud.

My body steeled itself for battle. I frantically began typing on my phone's keyboard. Words and long sentences with no punctuation poured out. I'd delete some text and add some more. There were so many things I wanted to say.

Barely keeping my eyes open, I put the phone down and went to bed, deciding it best to respond the next day.

The following day, I hadn't even thought of the comment until after I'd made myself a cup of tea and did a 10-minute meditation session.

I then remembered the message I had written out the night before. I decided my response would have been over the top and decided not to send it. Instead, I would contact this person privately and sort it out empathetically. I would not let this be a reason to feel attacked. I would let it be a reason for growth.

I opened my phone to locate the comment. When I read it again to figure out what to say, my eyes widened in embarrassment. The comment had not been an attack at all. It had been a compliment. In my sleep-deprived and exhausted state the night before, I had completely misread and misinterpreted what they had said (red).

I misinterpreted their message because of how I was feeling at the time I initially read it.

It's important to point out here that emotions are unique to you in terms of what makes you feel good or bad and will be based on your own unique experiences and observations. There is no wrong or right in terms of what should make you happy or not, nor should you chastise or overthink yourself over what does.

Through the principle of mirroring, we know that when we experience green light emotions, we will get back more green. Just as we can loop ourselves into red light cycles of dysfunction, we can also loop ourselves into green light circuits. In other words, well-being compounds.

When you are in green light states, you minimize chaos as a creative force in your life. This means you will come to experience less of it.

Of course, understanding our emotions and the way they make us feel are fundamental to what we experience and how we align to our creative core. You'll never entirely eliminate red light emotions. Telling someone "Just be happy" is easier said than done.

This is where the second most powerful tool of the alchemist comes in – the prefrontal cortex, aka: the human imagination – an engine built specifically for this purpose.

Intuition vs Fear

One of the tricky things about following our intuition – our internal guidance system – is that we often struggle to distinguish between fear and gut feelings. We have bad feelings about something and we confuse this with intuition. Or vice versa, we get a bad vibe and then talk ourselves out of it.

As a rule of thumb, it is easiest to understand that intuition is not communicated as a red light emotion. It is felt as a magnetism towards something or a repulsion (disinterest). Meaning, it is never felt as fear.

As a red light emotion, by default, fear is an invitation to reimagine the world. Intuition – on the flipside – represents a model of our world. Just like any red light, when we encounter gut feelings or intuition that feels like fear or dread, we should know we are no longer aligned to our creative core and the expanded version of ourselves. We must reframe. We must step back, recalibrate and reevaluate the situation from a green light space. Often when we do this, we don't react the same way we would have initially.

Astral Plane

I hear the whir of the night time insects. The lavender blades glow sliver under the light of the moon.

The soft padding of my feet against the dry earth scattered at the base of the willow, its dark looming shadow of a trunk shooting upwards, thick and muscular. Beneath the canopy, the light shines iridescent and twinkling in fireflies, just like the stars in the sky.

I'm inside a willow tree. I've been taking myself to this strange place inside my head lately. It was just one of the ways I was transmuting emotional states within myself. Here I could turn financial anxiety into calmness and confusion into acceptance.

The landscape was alien-like, but it felt safe.

Something beckoned me into the trunk, into the darkness. It was a pull I couldn't resist. I felt my feet move below as if on their own accord, my limbs numb and paralyzed of free will.

As I stepped inside, I discovered walls made of wet earth and crawling with roots. The temperature was cooler here and there was a smell of something earthly mixed in with the lavender hanging from the ceiling.

The only light came from a small cauldron in the middle that emitted a light shimmering all of the colors. Octarine. It threw the rest of the room into dark shadows. Centipedes and the poking heads of earthworms were not the only presence here.

I could feel someone, or something else in the room with me, though I could not see it at first. As my eyes adjusted to the dimly lit space, I began to make out a shape. A lone figure in the shadows stood with its back to me. Tall as if human but larger and with the curved posture of a witch.

I wondered if it knew I was there watching it, but I already knew the answer was yes by the way it held itself. A spider calculating through the lines of its web, the stiffness of a hand, the bending of an ear.

It turned towards me and revealed the wrinkled face of a turtle, large black blinking eyes and dreaded hair down to the floor. It called out, "Mum!"

Mum!

I'm jolted from my meditation by my daughter poking me with a jar of jam. The astral plane dissipated. "Mum! Can you open this for me, please?"

It had all felt so real and I knew I would return again soon.

15

SOURCE CODE: IMAGINATION

We suffer more in imagination than in reality.

— *SENECA*

In 30,000 BCE, a man enters a cave and by the flickering light of a tallow lamp, imprints the charcoal outline of a woman and a bison looming over her.

Almost thirty millennia later, in 1933, Pablo Picasso creates a piece with a striking resemblance.

While time and space separate the artists, it is clear that both had access to the same creative processing capabilities, otherwise known as the neocortex. Aka: the imagination.

The neocortex represents the largest portion of the brain and is a milky way of synapses made up of 16 million neurons.[1] Inside is the visual cortex, the auditory cortex, the somatosensory cortex, the motor cortex, and the posterior parietal region & prefrontal cortex.

In humans, the posterior parietal region and prefrontal cortex are especially enlarged. As a result, we can perform complex actions like using tools and have higher cognitive and creative capabilities than other animals.

This part of our minds allows us to set goals and imagine them by tapping into structures associated with emotions and memory.

It is also responsible for suppressing stimuli that are not relevant – creating the very reality tunnels from which we come to experience life through.

And because our perspectives determine the way we feel, they regulate every facet of our realities – what we buy, the clothes we wear, our cars, our friendships, or our enemies.

It's true that our five human senses are rather dull compared to other species - we cannot perceive electromagnetic waves with the naked eye nor can we smell the scent of a lingering footstep five years after the fact like our canine companions can but we do boast something far more spectacular than any other beast in the kingdom – human imagination. It is our superpower.

And you, my friend, are the owner-operator of such a magnificent device.

Of course, much like emotions, the imagination doesn't always feel like an ally. It's not a stretch to say that, for most of us, our imaginations work against us.

We worry about the economy or what might happen to our kids, our businesses, or our jobs. We imagine our partners leaving us or betraying us. We fabricate failures we're sure we'll encounter.

And because the human brain is a bona fide natural problem-solving machine that fixates on worst-case scenarios and issues at hand, the imagination, when left unmanaged, can spin us into circuits of the past. It stunts growth and pumps cortisol through our system.

It is both our salvation and the source of our suffering.

A good litmus test to tell if your imagination is working for or against you is to ask yourself: are you living mostly in red light emotions? If the answer is yes, then your imagination is not being used to its full capacity.

The true purpose and space of fulfillment of the creative core occur when we are intentionally and actively transmuting reds into green by using our imagination to imagine new, expanded realities. To invent and solve solutions, this is the process of creation.

For example, I recently interviewed someone for the podcast who complained that they were no longer fulfilled in their sixteen-year marriage because they felt frustrated and that they had lost their identity. It was clear from the red light that what they really desired was inner connection, support, and security (polarity of frustration).

When I asked them when the last time was that they experienced peace of mind, self-identity, and support it took them a long time to answer – too long. This is thus why the annoying husband trigger is showing up, because clearly this individual is trying to grow and expand but they lack the basic skill of providing themselves with the peace of mind and support that is required to help them receive what they seek.

Instead, they are waiting for the husband to change, and relying on what the husband says or does not say to validate them. But this is conditional well-being (when my husband behaves like XYZ, then I will feel happy, etc) and as we now understand, this approach never works and only pulls us deeper into chaos.

The task at hand is therefore for the individual to *imagine* the sensations of peace of mind and connection within themselves, to such a convincing level that it is thereby invoked into their realities. To teach themselves these states first – and then reality will solve/resolve/follow.

Our imagination is here to support our experience and expression of ourselves. It is also the reason why humans, above all else, are master storytellers.

Everything we do, from our media to our education to our mathematics and politics and the entirety of our lives, is one big story.

When we dive into new ideas, projects or businesses, we are effectively trying to improve the stories we tell around each one of these.

Sometimes we get really good at telling stories of how cash flows are going down, how it's other people's fault that we aren't succeeding, how money is hard to make, how we have no time, or how there are no good people out there.

We don't realize we are just enchanting and practicing/refining a story we are telling with our own life.

The story I got really good at telling myself was how I was trapped and unlovable.

So, the key to changing the circumstances of one's reality is the ability to change the story we tell about it, to narrate something entirely other than what is being perceived through the 3D physical reality, and to use our words to cast the spells to make it so. To do this, without question, you will need your imagination

Fortunately, because this superpower is innate, it is ours to command should we choose to.

Likewise, the world of alchemy proffers many techniques to help the alchemist accomplish the task of red light transmutations.

Some of my personal favorites include visualization, pathworking, memory recall, and invocations.

Here is a brief overview of each of these methods.

Visualization

Visualization is the process of bringing pictures into the mind's eye. The strange lavender landscape I was taking myself to in my meditations is one example of a visualization technique.

I imagined the virtual world and explored it in my head. When I started doing this exercise, I did not realize this was a form of magic. I just didn't want to be on earth any longer. Everything hurt, so I took myself somewhere else in my mind. And it worked.

The landscape was a mishmash of things I had observed or invented, two suns likely coming from Star Wars, the willow tree probably because there is a large willow in my own yard.

I would enter the landscape and walk through the field, feeling the flowers touch my skin and perceiving smells and sight and I would feel calmer, and more relaxed.

Imagining positive outcomes or imagined worlds, where we can abandon the physical machine for a moment, can help us transmute emotional states and place the feeling we desire in our bodies.

For example, if you identified that love was what you really desire, then you could imagine yourself in a world or visualize an experience where you are feeling loved.

Some people struggle to visualize images or visuals. If this is the case for you, just remember that sight is only one sense – enlist the help of the other senses to help you perceive an astral plane or experience.

Sometimes, I like to enlist the help of my other perceptual receptors to deepen a visualization, For example, if I am trying to find the space of love then I'll use jasmine or rose in the diffuser, and I'll tune into music or sounds that help pull me into imagined worlds and memories. Smell is handled by the olfactory bulb, and odors are passed on directly into the limbic system – the regions related to emotion.

Exercise – Create a Virtual World

Imagine a world or reality that you control that feels secure to you. It can be anything at all. Picture yourself stepping out of your own body, almost as if walking out of a machine and into this imagined world.

Create a place that feels safe, that feels ethereal, that feels like mysticism, that feels like magic.

Imagine that you are well, at ease, curious, secure, and confident. What is happening around you? Is it made of marshmallows or big pointed volcanoes? Are there others or are you solo? Don't judge it, just let your imagination create whatever it pleases, simply observe and know you are always looked after in this space.

This process should feel a bit like daydreaming – when you were a small child and imagining all the things you would like to be when you grow up. In your head, inventing ideas. These are the creative skills we should all aspire to.

The more you come back to this imagined space, the better you will become at surrendering and feeling into it. If it helps, you can also create kinesthetic prompts to assist with this mental shift. This is a method of neuro-linguistic programming (NLP), and is used to help call up desired emotional states within the body "on tap."

To achieve this, you essentially create a stimulus, such as touching your earlobe or your thumb and forefinger together, each time you visit your virtual world. The premise of this stimulus-response pattern is based on the famous conditioning experiments known as Pavlov's dogs. This experiment was fundamental in the field of psychology and resulted in the concept of classical conditioning.

At the time of placing the desired sensation in your body, create the prompt. This way – in the future – you will be able to simply touch this trigger to quick-start the shift.

This astral plane is your playground. It is a simulation of sorts, constructed within your own mind and can be used to create encounters with your intuition, aka spirit guides.

I would later come to learn, through a brief correspondence with the mage Peter Carroll, that the strange turtle creature I had encountered was a form of a spirit guide.

"I always regard them as part of myselves, maybe my future selves, rather than as traditional separate entities," he explained.

To guide yourself through spirit guides, center yourself back into green and consider the question, guidance, or clarity you seek – remember to keep it open-ended to avoid the ego muddling things up.

Remember to write down whatever guidance came through in your grimoire to keep a record of your encounters.

Pathworkings

A pathworking is a visualization technique that typically uses a story narrative and/or audio-visual prompts to create change within the mind. I first encountered this method of magic through the author Phil Hine in his book *Condensed Chaos* and it immediately became a favorite technique of mine.

In a guided pathworking, one person – the shaman – takes another through an astral plane. This can be especially beneficial if you are someone who struggles to sit and focus and needs the assistance of sensory cues and a storyline to pull you in.

Whereas most people try to clear their mind from thoughts during meditation (sensory deprivation), pathworkings, on the other hand, enlists the imagination to create encounters or new perspectives across astral planes.

To get the most out of pathworking, do it when you can really relax into the story and music. When you travel inside of your own mind, you want to be able to abandon your physical body for a moment. Park it somewhere you know will be safe and do it when you are in a good headspace.

As you begin playing around with more pathworkings, you will start to observe more flexibility in your own perspective. You'll encounter solutions and ideas where none previously existed.

Pathworkings are also a way to "charge" sigils (an inscribed or painted symbol considered to have magical powers - more on this later).

You can access free guided pathworking sessions at magicsourcecodes.com/training.

Memory Recall

Memory recall is another easy way to get our imaginations to transmute emotional states within ourselves. By remembering past experiences where we felt the feelings or sensations we seek, we can use our imaginations to restimulate those states within our bodies.

Here's a quick How To: Take two minutes to close your eyes and think back to a time in your life when you felt the way you want to feel now. For example, if you've identified abundance as the state you desire, think of a moment in your life when you felt abundant and experienced a moment of ease with money. Can you recall how this felt in your body and mind? What impact did it have on your perception of yourself and the world? Relive the experience in your mind to teach yourself the sensation once more.

If you have low self-worth and desire a state of worthiness, think of a moment when you felt worthy.

Obviously, this technique works best when you have actual memories available. I have met individuals who have told me they have never known a life without anxiety. They don't even know what "relaxed" or "at ease" feels like, so they have no muscle memory to go back to, making this technique more difficult to pull off. If this is the case for you, it's best to revert to imagining what it might feel like through an astral plane projection or virtual world, as discussed in the visualization technique.

Invocation

The biographical comedy *Man on the Moon* revolves around Jim Carrey's controversial invocation of the late Andy Kaufman. Such was his talent to mimic the comedian that it led to complete chaos during those months the movie was filmed. Jim Carrey remarks at the end, "I wonder what would happen if I held Jesus in my body for that long?" to testify to the technique's power.

Invocation is a process of holding a perspective in your own nervous system – their mannerisms, thoughts, posture, senses, etc. This is not dissimilar to what pathworking does, however, pathworkings are not necessarily around characters.

Once again, the imagination is key to pulling this off and the use of a kinesthetic prompt (such as wearing a mask or pinching your thumb to indicate a shift in perspective) can be useful here as well.

The best character to invoke is the future version of yourself that already possesses and embodies the life and traits you aspire to. I call this version You 2.0.

Imagine yourself as an actor tasked to mimic and mime the version of yourself that already has the money, the relationships, the health, and the life you seek. How do they act, think, talk, hold themselves, and behave? What are their posture and language like? What is their perspective on that unexpected invoice or bill or chaos showing up? The closer you can mimic their mannerisms and thought processes – the higher the probabilities will be stacked in your favor.

Sometimes it can be challenging to place the end feeling of wealth or love in your body or You 2.0 if you've never felt rich or loved by someone before. Invoking characters other than yourself can be helpful if this is the case.

For example, I often invoke Cleopatra. She was the wealthiest human of her time when she lived, a mighty stronghold for the feminine, and a practicing alchemist.

I will to view my reality through her lens and carry my body the way she would slide through hers. Through the invocation of her perspective, I build fluidity in my own.

At first, you will probably find it difficult to maintain a perspective for more than a few minutes and the exercise may even frustrate you. But remember, your imagination is just like any other muscle and strengthens through repetition and practice.

When I first began to play with invocations around wealth in the early days of growing my ad agency, the practice looked a bit like this:

- Meditate and place myself in the life of You 2.0 (in my imagination)
- Go test drive luxury cars
- Go to the open home of multimillion-dollar homes I couldn't afford
- Add ridiculously expensive items to online shopping carts (I couldn't afford to check out, but I would go through the whole online shopping experience and fool myself into believing I could afford those items)
- Walk around the marina of luxury yachts
- Giving bigger tips than I should have

- Said yes to things that didn't make much practical sense

It's important to note here that you should only push yourself financially through this invocation technique to a level that doesn't send you into deep reds of anxiety or panic. For example, technically speaking, the You 2.0 version of yourself may be flying first class and so invoking this version of yourself would invite you to match this as closely as possible by also flying first class. But this is not necessary and should not be attempted if doing so will place undue financial stress over you that you are not ready to transmute. If the invocation pushes you too much into a space of anxiety, it will defeat the purpose of the exercise. So while you may not be able to pay for the dream first-class tickets of You 2.0 you could certainly search for the seats online, act as you did, or even just pay for the airport lounge access instead. Once you begin to trust your own magical abilities more and you have gained the skills of transmutation of deep reds, then financial pressure can become an advantage. Until then, start with baby steps.

Invocation You 2.0

There is a version of yourself that already embodies all that you desire – they have the confidence, self-worth, and peace of mind, and operate within their creative cores, fully supported in abundant measures by life in the process.

They have what you are presently seeking or lacking now.

This version of yourself is mercurial in that it is continuously expanding and shifting. Never stagnating. Meaning that once you fulfill a desire, you will gain awareness of new ones. But because you operate from the standpoint of honoring these desires unconditionally (meaning you give yourself the state – using your imagination – before waiting for external reality to do it), this process is never exhausting. You find deep fulfillment in allowing and trusting yourself through growth.

Stepping into the perspective and thought processes of this version of yourself, You 2.0, as often and as closely as possible is key to changing the reflection to what you desire.

Embodying all you desire will conjure your own actions and behaviors accordingly. As a result, you'll change the very fabric of your reality.

Take a moment to consider the following about You 2.0:

What is different about their life from yours now?

What is their posture like?

What is their tone of voice?

What language or words do they use?

How do they move and interact with others?

How do they feel about (insert chaos)?

What does it feel like in your body, this expanded version of yourself?

Maybe it feels like your shoulders are a little bit back straighter.

Maybe it feels like a giddiness, like a bubbling inside that something is coming.

Perhaps it feels like surrendering and trusting. Ease.

Try it on for size, literally, pull that version of yourself into your skin and start walking around with it.

See if you can hold this perspective in your own body, even for just five minutes. Walk like the version of yourself living in that version of reality. Talk like them (this is more effective and enchants your own mind more effectively when this is done with strangers). Increase the stretches of time that you hold the perspectives in your own system. Can you do one hour? A half a day? Longer? The more you do this, the more you will pull your present self into that future probability.

16

CHANGING REFLECTIONS

Brriiiinnnnnnnnggg

My alarm went off. It was my thirty-fifth birthday and I'd decided to treat myself to a solo trek in the mountains. A little adventure.

It had been a month since the failed suicide attempt. I had become more perceptive to signs guiding and supporting me all around. I had also found a deep sense of flow by returning to the astral plane of pink skies and lavender fields.

The plant propagations had begun to take on their own rooting systems, and I transplanted them into bigger pots. I imagined them as embodiments of myself, cuttings of myself that were now growing anew, stronger. As the weather cleared the gardens outside began to take shape.

"Look," I called out to my son one day, as I held a broccoli leaf out to him. Hardly visible on the green leaf was a well disguised fat caterpillar, happily munching away, leaving behind large gapless chunks.

"Ah wow!" he exclaimed. The gift of children is that they are always so easily impressed. Wonder in their eyes. We both leaned in closer to observe the little critter, and as we did, a yellow wasp flew down and – without warning – ripped the caterpillar's head off clean, leaving only a writhing, chunky headless body behind.

My son and I reeled back in disgust and shock, both of us staring at the broccoli leaf dumbfounded, momentarily lost for words.

"Grosssssss! Did you see that mum!" his voice took on the tinge of morbid glee, "It ripped its head off, did you see that?"

"There you go, that's Mother Nature for you," I told him, watching the headless body curl up on itself as the little wasp returned to collect pieces of it. A reminder that "good" and "bad" were matters of perspective. I had settled into this knowing space, that the monster that had chased me down for so many years wasn't inherently bad. The strange turtle creature on the astral plane had even whispered the words omen into my ear and then showed me a reflection in a cauldron. I was beginning to understand that we were one and the same.

I was determined to change the reflection by changing the way I felt.

And so, for the past few weeks, I had started to track my daily emotional states by setting an alarm on my phone to ring every few hours during the day. Every time the alarm went off, I would "check in" with myself and note my mood down in a journal. It was the only way I knew how to continuously remind myself to snap out of red light emotional states.

I had become addicted to the circuits of depression. Feeling sad had been my modus operandus for so many years that I was hardly aware I was thinking sad thoughts when they happened. And so, the alarm reminder served to bring in conscious awareness. Whenever I heard the alarm, I'd do a self-scan – was I feeling good or bad?

When it felt not so great, I imagined myself flushing it out like a toilet. I'd picture the emotion vibrating through my body, the sensation, and then I imagined it flowing out of me. At first, my mind fought this exercise. It wanted to desperately focus on all the fires and flames, but with more intention, it became easier to dull it out. I got faster and better at "flushing" out red.

When it was deep red: anger, panic, or depression, I would say "fuck it" and just surrendered and allowed it to exist. This made it easier to flush it out.

I tried to prioritize activities to help me feel well and get me back into green.

Some days, I ran around a lake. Or I sat on a paddleboard and smoked weed. Other days, I dove my head into the waves of the ocean and let the salt dry on my skin. Some days still, I did nothing at all and just lazed around.

I did these activities on a rotating basis, not always in consecutive order.

And at the end of each day, I reviewed my emotional state journal entries. I circled a blue dot with that day's average and connected it to the previous days with a line on a paper graph.

It looked like the outline of the titanium jaws of destiny

I had used a similar technique for manifesting money in my business a few years back with success. The exercise was based on the principle of Pearson's Law – "*That which is measured improves.*" I figured if it worked for money, it would probably also work with emotions. I had nothing to lose.

Brrriniiiiiingggg, briiiiiiiinggggggg

The alarm went off again, and I ran a last scan before getting ready to leave for my big birthday outdoor adventure. The trek I'd planned was supposed to follow the ridge of a peninsula that led to a solo lighthouse with some bunk beds where I could stay the night. I felt nervous but also excited, the air of the adventurer about.

What was becoming clear in the little dots taking form was that I was a girl living with a lot of fear and regrets.

I was too easily spooked – tell me there's another pandemic wave and I'm buying a twelve pack of toilet paper.

The counter of fear is courage and play, and so here I was heading off into the unknown.

Do I have my compass? I searched through the front pocket of my pack just to double-check.

The last time I had been hiking alone, I had found myself lost and panicked. It had been this trip where I'd learned that a compass without a map is useless. I was prepared this time, with a screenshot of the trail on my phone, a printed map, a compass, and even an emergency blanket – I wasn't going to take any risks.

I stuffed the last item in the top of the bag, a large can of condensed coffee. It was impractical, but one of my little pleasures – having a warm cup of the sugary stuff while I watched the sunrise, dressed in my fleece onesie.

Nuts, ramen noodles, protein bars, and a big goon bag, as the Australians would call it – of wine – to celebrate my birthday at the top of the mountain under the night sky. Just myself and the cosmos.

Certain I had everything I needed, I grabbed my stuff and headed out to the car. As I heaved my heavy pack into the boot of the car, the skies suddenly opened, and rain began to pour.

Fuck!

I ran to the driver's seat, drenched in moments. Started the car and turned on the wipers that could barely keep up with the pelting of rain.

Think, think, think.

A hike in this kind of weather wasn't going to work, but the trail was still a six-hour drive up north – there was time and space yet for it all to clear.

Ok, this isn't the end, I tell myself optimistically

I pulled out of the driveway and slowly peeled out into the road, leaning forward to see through the grey slate.

I was lost in my thoughts when the check engine light turned on, a small menacing glowing orange din against the dashboard. I'm not a car person, but I knew this wasn't a good sign just before a six-hour drive. Undeterred, I pulled into a gas station.

Turns out it was the oil that needed topping up. After pouring a new bottle in and wiping off the excess I had spilled, I slam the boot of the car down and hit the road once more.

This time feeling puffed through my chest with pride. Here I was, facing all these things going wrong and I was handling it like a pro, water off my back, and now the check engine light is gone and I'm a real car whisperer.

Ha, check me out, I gloated to myself silently, *I am a master mechanic.*

I felt like a million dollars.

On the stereo, a podcast was playing at random. I listened in as a man called Dr. Dean Radin was being interviewed.

"What's really fascinating is this study was showing how the majority of these scientists had confessed to experiencing supernatural phenomena and holding a belief in magic, but it is career suicide to admit to it…"

Suddenly the car began to jolt and kick back. An enormous plume of white smoke came out of the hood, and the car abruptly slowed to a crawl. Around me, cars and trucks whizzed past, splashing sheets of water across my windshield as they went by. I felt like Mr. Bean driving thirty kilometers per hour on the freeway. I pulled over on the side of the motorway and got out of the car to inspect the engine, but it was futile. I had no idea what I was looking at and the unrelenting rain had me shivering within moments.

The hiking trip was wishful thinking at this stage. I squeezed myself back into the passenger seat and re-evaluated my options.

Two hours later, after getting the car back to a repair shop, it was dark outside, and I was drenched. The taxi dropped me off at the front of my house, cold and wet.

As I unpeeled my clothing and sought out warmth in the home, the power suddenly cut out and I was plunged into pitch blackness.

Great, I think to myself, but my mood is still high.

I set up a little makeshift campsite on my bed. My bones shake beneath the fleece and blankets from hours of exposure to the cold.

The camp light casts shadows on the walls. I grabbed a yellow packet of noodles from my pack and broke the little flavor packet and poured it over the noodles.

Happy birthday to me.

I couldn't help but shake my head at what had happened over the course of the day.

Everything that could have gone wrong, did.

I was alone, soaking wet, and in the dark on my birthday.

And yet, across the room from me, is the unmistakable gleam of a cheek in the reflection of a mirror. The reflection was smiling back.

I was happy despite it all.

The Alchemist

I am the Alchemist.

Made of stardust and a thousand lightning bolts

Inside my eyes swirls a galaxy that is both quantumly and precisely the same size as a speck of dust

My body is lined with the roots of a million trees, veins that pump instructions of a higher code

In each heartbeat, the dusting of octarine

Look closer, into my soul

And you may come to see your own

I am the one who declares themselves the path of least resistance

A warrior of consciousness

To find my own hand in the bible black night

Calibrating to clarity even in obscurity

In each breath, the tales of a billion past lives are told

I feel it all, I have felt it all

The riches, the love, the expansion, the despair, the pain, the disgrace, the suffering

All of it is me

And none of it is me

I am the Alchemist

And I lead the way

17

LOVE LIFE

The spell was to conjure love.

Because I was finally ready.

It had been two months since I'd intentionally begun to use my imagination to transmute emotional states and track my daily emotions. Three months since the last suicide attempt.

I had found my smile again. I was able to banter with all that had gone down, all that had been lost, and now what I desired was to receive love.

The ritual called for 108 beads to create the mandala necklace. The instructions were that – with each bead threaded through – I was to place my focus on my desired relationship.

I sat down on the couch, arranging the rose quartz beads and string in front of me.

Pink is an interesting color as there is no single wavelength of this tone. It cannot occur naturally in nature without the bending of a rainbow, the mingling of red and violet. In plants, the pigmentation of pink leaves indicates a loss of chlorophyll, the result of a mutation that means the plant can no longer turn sunlight into sugar properly.

Pink is magic.

I picked up the first bead and tried to stab the cotton string through the bead's impossibly small hole, my tongue sticking out, but the ends frayed no matter how many times I licked it.

Finally, the thread pushed through the little glossy bead. Only 107 more to go!

I imagined myself feeling loved, well, safe, and excited. Worthy. At first, this was a difficult state to place myself in, but with each little bead, the sensation was easier and easier to call upon.

I saw octarine in the swirl of my eyes – beyond the body, the business, the bank account, and the relationships.

I worked to make myself feel loved and worthy without the prince charming…

I went deep into my virtual world to find a sense of purpose…

Each little bead brings me back to this place.

The more I did this, the easier it became.

Only 76 beads left to go.

And then, magic happened.

For the first time in a long time, I felt well. Like, really well.

Not just smiling, but full inside. Bursting and brimming with gratitude and appreciation.

The depressive thoughts now seemed far away and alien. They no longer hovered over my shoulder, waiting to interject into my days.

This would have gone unnoticed if it wasn't for my little graph and the little pinprick dots scribbled across. A trend. An upswing. Clear as day, there it was in the outline.

Little dots are meaningless on their own, but together they formed an entire universe for me. A little circle was sketched out across the Y-axis for seven and then another one the next day.

Hitting another day above a five was a win for me. Scoring seven two consecutive days seems like no big deal, but to me, it meant everything. For the first time in a long time, I was managing full days without thinking of killing myself once. Full days that turned into full weeks.

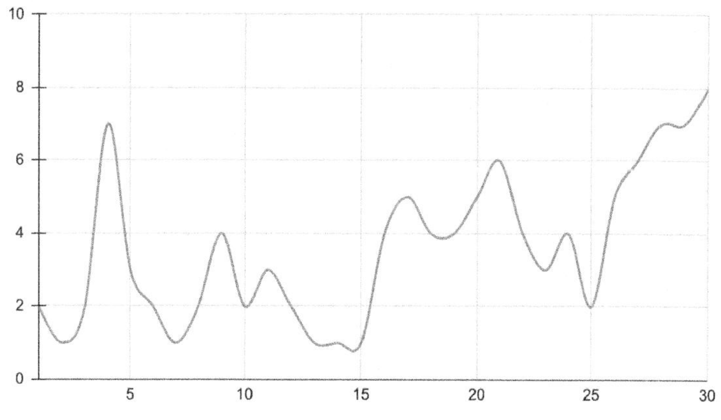

For the first time in a long time, I didn't hate myself. I was actually really proud of the woman I had become. I felt gratitude for the chaos that had been.

Some interesting things had also started to come to pass in my life. Solutions and unexpected opportunities were coming out of the least expected places.

Past clients and students of mine reached out to negotiate the sale of my company. It presented itself without effort on my part.

I relocated to a beautiful home in the country that had come up randomly in a hot seller's market below my budget.

Somehow, money flowed through from unexpected places to always ensure I was covered for my needs.

It was like the more I detached from the problems, the more all the issues that existed were solving themselves in the most serendipitous of ways.

Only 52 beads to go.

I licked the end of the string and tried to loop another bead through, but it was impossible. The string needed to be trimmed with every new bead. This was my third attempt at completing it, the first two times beads had been lost and sacrificed under the kitchen counter.

My phone buzzed. It was a friend.

Come have a drink at mine! Pleaaseeee.

I wasn't really in the mood but needed a break from the necklace, and I was starting to go cross-eyed trying to complete it.

I placed the necklace on the bookshelf in a little brown bag to prevent all the loose beads from straying.

Screw it. The necklace could wait. I was happy being single, possibly for the first time in my life.

Later that night, while the pink beads glistened like wet roses waiting for the crescent moon in the brown paper bag, I saw a pink aura around a man in a basement bar and fell in love.

Ritual of Love

This simple ritual uses a candle to help draw your focus into the invocation of your ideal relationship.

Consider what does it feel like in your body to be in a safe, thrilling, and loving relationship? How does it change the way you perceive your surroundings?

Stare into the flame for twenty minutes and hold this perspective and version of reality.

To enhance the effects of this ritual, apply physical changes within your environment that indicate the relationship status. For example, when I did this, I carried out the following:

I made space in my closet for my future partner's clothes…

I dated myself…

I treated and talked to myself the way I wanted a partner to…

I left little love notes around the house for myself as I would wish a partner to do for me...

Sigils

Sigils are a symbolic representation of intentions. They were coined by Austin Osman Spare and are an easy way to craft our desires into reality.

In *The Book of Pleasure*, Spare describes the process of sigilation as follows:[1]

"*Enshrine your desire in a short sentence; write out the sentence and then put down all the individual letters of which it is composed, omitting any repetition of a letter. When the sentence has been reduced to a minimum number of letters, unite them graphically in one composite glyph which does not suggest the nature of the desire. Then — and this is of great importance — forget the desire and sink the sigil in the subconsciousness.*"

These "alphabets of desire" are similar to hieroglyphics often created as monograms. An interesting thing about hieroglyphs is that they are the only written language that can be read both up and down and left to right. It takes lateral thinking to read the ancient scrolls.

Once you overcome preconceptions of alchemy and magic, you realize that sigils are powerful in that they pull the focus in by engaging the creative faculties of the mind. This also doubles as a way to get you into a state of flow – one to the high alchemy states, which we will explore in more detail in later chapters.

The cool news about sigils is they can take on almost any tactile experience you desire – from molding clay balls to body paint on yourself or a sexual partner. What materials help you step into flow – wood, paper, sketches, ice, dirt, or plants? Use those. There is no right or wrong and the practice of alchemy is very much a practice of self-exploration.

Example sigil I made up for the intent of completing this book. Can you see how it incorporates the letters M and S and a C shape in a serpent? It is a monogram of the original intent.

The first step to creating a sigil is to write down the intention. For example, in the picture below, the intention was to foster community and accountability. The letters are pulled together and mashed to form a symbol. The final symbol wouldn't mean much to people looking at it, but my subconscious understands what it represents.

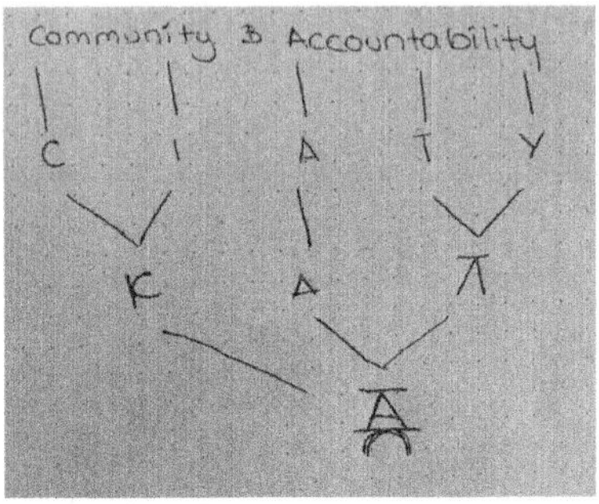

CHARGE THE SIGIL

Charging a sigil just means imprinting the intent by placing your focus on the sigil during a moment of altered consciousness (gnosis). Altered consciousness can be achieved most commonly through sensory overload, sensory deprivation, orgasm, breathwork, and hallucinogens. We will be discussing gnosis in more detail soon.

"BANISH"/RELEASE THE INTENTION

The second most important ingredient to successful alchemy, next to the creative imagination, is belief/trust. Once a conjuring is done, the magic is released to be taken care of and allowed to do so without your questioning focus. This is often referred to as "banishment" or "releasing" and is the most challenging part of the whole process.

For this reason, place the sigil you have created somewhere relatively out of sight, somewhere you will only cross occasionally.

After creating many, many sigils, your conscious mind will come to forget the meaning of the specific sigils and their corresponding intentions over time. This is actually a good thing because it won't prompt you to be perceptive if it has not yet come to pass.

This is another reason I strongly recommend you record all your magic in a special journal for this purpose only – so that one day you may refer back to what you did and see for yourself the power that is You in plain sight.

18

SOURCE CODE: BANISHMENT

When there is no anxiety to reach a particular destination, there is an opportunity for adventure.

— LYANDA LYNN HAUPT

My experience of dating and finding love at that point in my life had felt difficult. When I was deeply lonely, I desired so badly to have someone to love. I went on hundreds of dates and just came across brick walls. It felt so easy for everyone else, but for me, somehow, I was broken. I was catfished and ghosted and all but deleted and downloaded the dating apps a million times. Gradually, this loneliness also fed into the depression that broke the camel's back.

I was so desperate after a while that I even went as far as purchasing the domain sugarmamonthehunt.com (don't ask)!

It was like the more I desired it, the harder and more impossible it seemed that it would ever happen to me.

And then, suddenly, the moment I stopped caring and became happy being single for the first time in my life, I found love almost instantly. Oh, the irony. An experience many of us can relate with.

This was also my experience with pregnancy in my first marriage. The times we tried to conceive felt long and frustrating, with me taking vitamins and eating healthy. Lying down with my legs over my head and taking my temperature each morning. Both conceptions occurred after giving up and getting drunk.

It's so easy to manifest the free parking space or random tax returns, but when it comes to the stuff we truly, deeply desire, it can seem like we can't give ourselves what we want.

The reason for this goes back to mirroring and red light states. If we are aware something is lacking, we are essentially displeased with present circumstances, which means we are making our well-being conditional. It feels like a longing, a missing, a burning desire that pains us and consumes our focus.

By pining for it in such a way, we inadvertently fall out of our creative cores and are now inviting chaos to bring us back to ourselves. More loneliness, more spinning wheels. More frustration, more hopelessness.

When we are displeased with present circumstances, we must enlist the help of our imagination to fool ourselves into believing it is already being taken care of. It is coming.

A passive expectation, a deep sense of calm in the body that all is taken care of for you.

You can understand why this is also the hardest part of the entire process of alchemy.

Try telling someone who is lonely to stop thinking about how lonely they are.

Try telling someone who desperately desires to have a baby to stop thinking about babies.

Or the person with looming bankruptcy to not obsess over the shortage of money.

Easier said than done.

Again, the brain is hardwired to fixate on problems. When there is a perceived gap in our desired circumstances, our brains lock and load themselves to aggressively solve for it. Getting the horse's head to turn is the master sign of the alchemist

So how can banishment effectively be achieved?

Gnosis provides a powerful way to do exactly that

Nature & Divine Timing

Adopt the pace of nature, her secret is patience - Ralph Waldo Emerson

One of the big reasons I found pleasure in gardening at this time in my life was that I began working with a different time dimension.That is, nature's timeline. In nature, things have their own pace. The fly dies within a day, the seedling grows over months, and the oak takes a lifetime.

When we feel impatient over the results of our efforts to craft intentions into reality, we can allow the divine timing of nature to take it off our hands.

What You'll Need

Pen & paper

Seedling of a flower

Soil

Pot

How to Do

You can choose to light a white candle and inscribe the intention across it. Light it to indicate the start and end of the ritual.

On the paper, write out what your desired intention is. Next imagine it so that by the time the plant flowers, your wish will be delivered.

Bury the intention in a pot, place soil over it, and bury the seedling. Nurture and care for the seedling, but beyond that, do not obsess over how much it has grown in a day. Let it develop as nature intended it to.

TIP - I love variegated plants like the pink princess for this type of ritual. I often do this conjuring with propagations of a mother plant (a process that can take 5-6 months before the plant even puts out full leaves). I first place the cutting in water for it to root, then when it has a good network of roots, I place it in soil. The intention manifests itself once the plant produces another full pink leaf (pink princess), or half white leaf in the case of the monstera. Using variegated plants in this way is more immersive because the leaf mutations are not guaranteed and happen randomly, meaning you are accepting a timeframe of potentially 1-2 years for your manifestation to come to pass – or potentially not at all.

Again, the point is not that we are telling ourselves that it will necessarily take two years or never happen but that we allow this probability to exist knowing full well the timing and what is received will always be perfect. When we step into this resonance, ironically we make it come to ourselves faster. This is the power of releasing.

19

GNOSIS

A Mesolithic man, debilitated by blood-bloated ghosts swarming through his veins, lies in the center of a cave. Above him, a female shaman wearing antlers and a head-dress of feathers crushes berries and herbs inside a tortoise shell.

As she moves about the small space, her hips jingle with the bones of rabbit tails and a human foot. A drum beats steadily away, reverberating through the cave.

The shaman pours the dark liquid into the hunter's mouth to expel the spirit that has made him ill. A low gurgle escapes from her throat. As the man lays still in a cold sweat, she enters a trance, her eyes rolling back, her body stiffening. She uses a drum to further enhance the effect of distended reality, chanting in tongues, and making a show of fighting off the evil force in his blood.

The shaman is no longer of this earth.

Gnosis.

The word gnosis stems from the Greek term meaning "knowledge" and refers more specifically to a kind of intuitive, nondiscursive, salvational knowledge of one's own true self and of God.

It is employed by magicians to seal intentions into the subconscious, bypassing the regular cognitive controls of the mind.

The more typical approaches to achieving gnosis in the world of alchemy include:

1. Sensory deprivation – such as meditation or float tanks.
2. Breathwork – such as hyperventilation or connected breathwork (check out the book *Life Force* by Dave Lee for more on this approach) is an easy way to change emotional states within the body.
3. Orgasm – a personal favorite of most chaos magicians, also could fall under sensory overload. Bring the sigil/intent to mind at the moment of orgasm.
4. Sensory overload – chanting and drumming, psychedelics, pathworkings, or even multi-sensory environments such as arcades.

Exhaustion and physical duress are also popular choices of magicians. A ten-day fast was common practice amongst ancient Egyptian priests and priestesses to induce states of trance. They used this energy to channel and recite carefully instructed invocations, words that reverberated through the body so that they could call upon the gods and goddesses themselves. The whole process intended to deepen the potency of the spells cast.

Following the red/green light system, however, it is preferable to avoid any method of gnosis that is based on or causes red light. It's true that pain and exhaustion can be a great gateway into the cosmos, but equally so too can love.

Sex magic, which happened to be my first unintentional use of gnosis for purposes of crafting my reality, was a popular favorite of the ancient Greeks. Around one-quarter of ancient tablets found showed erotic magic being used as revenge or to bind a lover.[1]

I had first heard about sexual transmutation through the work of Napoleon Hill in *Think and Grow Rich* four years after starting my agency.

I would use toys on myself and think about how good it felt to receive the success and freedom I desired.

A few years on from this I would come to experience sex magic in a group context, this time at Burning Man during a performance from an LA shamanic circus band.

There were ten of us who had been picked out from the crowd lying down on the stage in a circle. The crowns of our heads towards the onlookers who shifted eagerly in their cushions. Anticipation hung in the air, a long-lashed girl looking up.

Above us, dangling down, a half-naked woman was distended and contorted around a silk rope.

"Breathe!" the shaman had instructed us, "BREATHE," he roared, expanding his chest, arms outstretched. The crowd and all of us on the stage had taken a collective breath in.

That's when I started to feel it, the tingling in my legs, moving up like electricity, into my genitals like a bolt of lightning, a heat and a spark all at once. My body spasmed, contorting with pleasure and laughter as if it touched the synaptic ends of a lightning bolt.

Orgasm powered by electricity. A plug attached to a socket, an orgasm powered by a force within. All ten of us had experienced the same thing at once.

Studies show that at the time of orgasm, the lateral orbital cortex of the brain shuts down, and dopamine and oxytocin activate spatially remote parts of our minds, reducing fears and anxiety. This induces a similar chemical response to listening to your favorite music or being in deep flow states.

At that time, my business was at its peak, breaking milestone after milestone. I was being recognized globally for my work and had grown a follower base in the industry. I was confident and sure-footed even though half the time, what I did was crazy and nonsensical. I traveled the world often and always flew business or first class.

While it wouldn't be honest to say that masturbating was the sole reason I made millions, it played (pun intended) a part.

Hallucinogens are another way to access states of gnosis and were often used in ancient civilizations. In *The Immortality Key*, Brian C Muraresku explores the Mysteries of Eleusis, the longest-running and most prominent spiritual tradition of ancient Greece that spanned from 1500 BCE to 392 CE, after which the party was outlawed by the Christian Emperor Theodosius.[2] The priestesses of the

Eleusis used an elixir called *kykeon* believed to have contained traces of parasitized ergot, a powerful psychoactive fungus that grows on barley (mimics LSD (acid) effects). The drink was the only drink the goddess Demeter would accept in the reenactment of Persephone's abduction by her uncle Hades.

And while hallucinogens and orgasms are effective ways to induce altered consciousness, there are three naturally occurring emotional states that stimulate similar results that the magician can tune into at any moment.

Sex Magic: Try it Out Yourself

The Hindus used tantra as sex magic while the Kabbalists saw sex as a way to draw down blessings from above. In the world of alchemy, sexual energy is said to come from the Kundalini, the power center of the body.

When sexual energy is mixed in with consciousness, it enables us to create mind to matter, making us like honey to a bee of our intentions.

The way to perform sex magic is fairly simple – bring yourself to a state of arousal, and at the time of orgasm, bring the intention or desire to focus. If you have a sigil, this is when you would want to look at it.

If you're a man, be sure not to ejaculate as you will release this potent creative energy (this is why it is recommended to professional athletes not to have sex the night or day before big games – sexual energy is powerful!). The female can multiply energy by multiplying orgasms.

Almost immediately, you will begin to experience increased magnetism for people, solutions, ideas, and answers. You may notice people begin to look at you differently and become more responsive and aware of you.

When I perform this, I will use toys on myself, although ideally, it's best if you try to arouse yourself through your imagination and thought alone.

This shows true mastery of the imagination. Can you bring yourself to near orgasm and please yourself in such a way using only the tool inside yourself with no other stimuli? It might not come easily at first, but again, the imagination strengthens the more it is practiced.

As the heat builds in my body, I imagine pulling the energy upwards into my mind, mixing the snake with consciousness. I picture the energy rising from my sexual organs to power a generator within.

At the moment of climax, I will think about my sigil and intention. I place the feeling space of what I desire and mix it in with the beautiful energy of gnosis.

Try it Out as a Couple

The theorist Paschal Beverly Randolph once said of this method "At the instant of intense mutual orgasm, the souls of the partners are opened to the powers of the cosmos, and anything truly willed is accomplished."

Take this a step further by involving your partner in the conjuring. Draw each other's sigils on each other (a non-permanent marker of course) and look at the sigils across each other's bodies as you are having sex. My partner did this to me by drawing his sigil across my chest – his desire came into reality no more than six months later.

20

RED LIGHTS

The man in the basement bar with the pink aura and I fell in love.

Afternoons at the tepid baths together, weekends watching movies, evenings cooking for one another.

He has an unspellable name and watches me shave my pussy in the shower. I draw little hearts on the mist against the glass. All the while, the pink beads from my love spell still unfinished in their paper bag.

Everything in my life had taken on a different pace, a lightness of being. My emotional chart felt like the softness of air-dry sheets on a summer's day. I had sold the company and I had fallen in love. Life was abundantly more giving and easier than before. Things that had felt difficult before now came to me with seeming ease.

And – most importantly – the monster had stayed away.

I was finally in a safe relationship with myself.

I would get lost watching the veins throb on his arm, the heat rising in my own body. Salacious thoughts that sent me into a world of play.

A shadow pulling over his face.

A flower stamen deep in the bowl.

A bee sucking in hallucinated pleasure.

Underwear tight against my thighs.

A growth in his groin.

A snake coming to carve out my insides.

Echoes that sliced through memories the same way a lazy breeze blows through the cutty grass.

At times, I felt myself observing this new reality as something foreign, alien, and put together at the fringes. That at any moment now, everything might just come apart.

It almost felt too good to be true. Too smooth and easy.

A little voice in my head would question when it would all come crashing down.

You really think you deserve all this? It would taunt. *Fat chance. You will walk away with your heart broken again.*

A part of me couldn't believe that I deserved all that was happening. It was like I was half expecting it all to be taken away from me at any moment, like somebody would pop out from a Truman box and yell, *Surprise!*

After two years of disconnection from receiving from my creative core, accepting it could be easy was a struggle.

Even the addiction to overwhelm proved a real difficulty to overcome. I found myself chastising myself and shaming myself for spending the days gardening or writing.

What are you doing?... You should be productive... You're wasting your time... These were the words I would often repeat to myself.

One night, this internal unease manifested itself right in the middle of my partner's living room. A small flat that he shared with a friend. He had just come out of the shower and was preparing a protein shake for himself and I was sitting on the edge of his bed, a small room with the Tao and a small white crystal I'd gifted him on the bedside table.

I was supposed to stay the night at his house, but panic started to grip me. The voice of doubt grew louder.

It – matter of factly – reminded me of the heartbreak, all the past failures, and all the times I have felt hurt.

Of my eighteen-year-old self being dumped and heartbroken, of my last breakup and how I had stood in the kitchen sobbing to his words.

My heart rate rose, and every signal in my body told me to walk out and leave.

"I'm so sorry," I told him through tears as I grabbed my keys and hurriedly left his place, leaving him standing in the kitchen, half-naked and confused.

I had a tendency to do this: just walk away or sabotage the good things in my life because the thought of being hurt or losing it was too great. It's easier to walk away. As miserable as I had been single, it was easier than having to face *that* again. It was easier to stick to the comforts of the known misery.

And now, this pattern was rearing its head again. I saw a happy version of myself and replayed the rolling tapes of all the tears that had followed those last times.

It was dark outside, and the street was quiet as I crossed over to my parked car, pulling a sweater over myself. My entire body was hijacked in panic.

As I slid the car into gear, I felt my stomach drop the further away I drove. I felt sad to leave him behind. My jaws steeled. This was for my own good, I told myself.

The motorway on-ramp was ahead of me, and thoughts rolled over each other in my mind. Something else seized me, a realization that if I left now, I would lose him. I pulled over and sat frozen in my car for what must have been an hour, the indicator light ticking away in the background. A war was being waged inside. The universe seemed to pull up, like a horse at a high fence.

Then, another little voice, barely detectable. Pointing out the obvious with sweeping clarity. I was running away because of fear.

Fear.

Red light.

Every fiber in my body felt compelled to sprint, like a gazelle in the path of a lion. But I realized then, with the steam building on the windows, that it was all an invitation, an illusion.

I knew what needed to be done.

I turned the car around and drove back to his place.

Courage.

Transmutation.

21

SOURCE CODE: HIGH ALCHEMY STATES

A high alchemy state is a naturally occurring state of gnosis – a form of altered consciousness – that places you back into your co-creative core.

These states are powerful enough to shift your focus away from the inner critic and obsessive focus, breaking red light circuits.

They naturally help you to re-engage and tap into worthiness and deservedness. They naturally open you up to receiving without having to try to shove beliefs down your own throat.

When we cannot stop thinking about the thing we really desire, when we cannot stop noticing how we are not where we desire to be, the high alchemy states assist us in commanding the head of the horse, so to speak.

They hold you to your creative core. They allow you to banish spells and prevent you from confusing the information signals sent out and received. And the best part is that they are naturally occurring. They are the baseline of your being.

The three high alchemy states are:

1. Love
2. Play
3. Flow

All three replicate the states of consciousness achieved through orgasm, hallucinogens, or sensory deprivation – gnosis

They captivate your attention and make you nearly deaf to the inner critic inside, or at the very least, resilient to it.

When we fall in love, for example, we ignore all the advice of friends and family and the red flags. We are captivated fully by the experience.

When we are in a state of flow, surfing the waves, or doing a yoga class, we are not thinking about how unworthy we are. We are not thinking about the problems in our life.

And likewise, when we are in a state of play, courageously scaling the face of a mountain or our belly hurting from laughter, we are not worried about looming bills or the economy.

We are completely present, accepting, and grounded within our creative core.

The reality is that most of us grow up believing that these states exist outside of ourselves, instead of actually being a part of us. We feel disconnected, and lonely and frustrated because we have beliefs and perceptions that have led us to forget these states ARE us.

As we have explored before, it doesn't matter what gets us into these states, whether it's actual activities of physical experiences or our imaginations. Our nervous system cannot tell the difference. We have the capacity to transmute play, flow, and love within ourselves because it is the core of our creative being and, therefore, always accessible to us regardless of external validation or conditions.

And because these states are rooted in the creative core, they minimize chaos. They create green light ripple effects throughout their own realities. They self-reinforce circuits of green.

Those of you reading this who have experienced financial success can probably attest that the money flowed most easily when you were deeply passionate and excited by what you were creating. Flow is a magnet to money because money is simply a representation of value and when we are grounded to our creative cores, in flow, it is easier to both provide value and value ourselves.

They are called high alchemy states because they place you back into the easy stream of life. As Abraham Hicks often says. Following the current of life instead of going against it is the key to receiving desires.

When you are in a high alchemy state, you attract more money, more clients, more opportunities, more solutions, better relationships, and better ideas. Things come to you with little effort. Doors open and life serves you her cornucopia.

Setting intentions when we are in a high alchemy state is one of the fastest ways to call what we desire to ourselves.

Here's a breakdown of each one of these states.

Flow

Flow is the sensation of immersed focus and distortion of time. It is felt as a creative compulsion and deep focus within the body. The inner critic and mental chatter are quieted, novel ideas are born, and random associations collide. The effects are a loss of self-consciousness, the distortion of time, and the autotelic experience.

The duality of flow is overwhelm because when you are in flow, you can work twelve-hour days and barely feel it, whereas when you are overwhelmed, a three-hour stint will drain you of life. And so, when we find ourselves overwhelmed, we can transmute the state through the "prescription" of flow.

What gets you into a state of flow is unique and varied to you and could include writing, painting, exercise, music, dancing, singing, friends, sex, etc. I once worked with a client whose favorite pastime was cleaning bathrooms! This activity placed her into deep flow and peace of mind.

If you aren't sure what gets you into this high alchemy state, now is a good time to start exploring and building up your toolkit. Try different things out; the more you have up your sleeve, the easier the journey into magic.

Rituals are a proven way to enter states of flow and although research is fairly new regarding the psychological effect of rituals (until recently, rituals were the domain of anthropology), studies provide relatively strong support that they regulate negative emotions and enhance creativity.[1] They focus attention away from deficit emotions (red light) and block out intrusive thoughts.

Rituals were one of the big pulling cards that drew me into the world of alchemy.

During the performance of a ritual, focusing on the series of action sequences such as burning a letter of intent, inscribing sigils across wax, or rolling clay into a wish ball provides tactile, visual, and kinesthetic components that further draw the focus in.

I burned letters. I buried seedlings over intentions. I released ashes into the ocean and inscribed desires on wax. I used my own understanding of how I like to learn and create and customized rituals accordingly.

The good news is that you don't need to make a milk offering to a goddess to be able to use rituals as a way to immerse yourself into this high alchemy state. Incorporating elements that hold the meaning of symbolism to you is enough.

Magic is all about meaning.

And for this reason, there is no right or wrong way to do a ritual – it all works as long as it provides you with a creative booster.

Take a moment to list out and consider the activities that place you into a state of flow. Think of other activities beyond these that you have not yet tried that you suspect you may also enjoy.

Ritual: Creating a Wishball

A wish ball is a clay representation of an intention. It is one of my favorite types of rituals because working with clay is a tactile experience that operates much like squeezing a stress ball. It naturally relaxes us and assists us in deepening our focus by placing us into flow.

What You'll Need

- Air-dry clay

- Essential oil

If you are conjuring for specific outcomes (such as a revenue level or outcome in a business), wait until you are in green light. If you attempt this ritual while in red light, set an intention of well-being and the ultimate desired state.

Use essential oil drops in the clay, and choose the scent that symbolizes the intent. For example, lavender could be used for self-worth, jasmine or rose for love, peppermint for sex and creative energy, or eucalyptus for healing.

Begin to heat the clay in your hands. As you do, consider a symbolic shape that represents your intentions and begin to mold it in the clay. There is no right or wrong here. Keep your focus on the intent as you are sculpting it.

Let the clay dry and then 'banish' the intent to your alchemy box or somewhere you won't see daily.

Play

Pay attention to young mammals coming into this world and you will observe that they enter in a state of awe and playfulness. Babies, puppies, and lambs are all playful by nature. Life, or consciousness, operates naturally in a high alchemy state. The state is synonymous with happiness and serves to develop pro-social skills as well as the part of the brain responsible for high-order thinking.[2] As such, the young mammalian brain is programmed and motivated to engage in playful behaviors, with adverse consequences of "faulty wiring" and impaired emotional and cognitive skills when these attempts are thwarted.

Unfortunately, despite play being key to brain plasticity and a powerful form of trauma therapy, most adults lose their sense of playfulness through past failures, traumas, rejections, and other negative experiences. Not to mention the decline in free play with over-scheduled kids, smaller backyards, and increased screen time, which all lead to higher depression and anxiety rates.

In our modern-day and fast-paced world, play is de-prioritized with devastating mental health consequences.

The sensation of play feels like an expression of giddiness, lightness, and courage in the body and can be experienced through imaginative means, rough and tumble, and adventure. It is the dual of fear and anxiety because when we're playing, we're resilient to fear and anxiety. We can bungee jump and try new things without giving a second thought to fear. Accordingly, when we are in deep states of anxiety or fear, the most powerful way to transmute the red circuit is to use the antidote of play and courage as I did the night I turned the car around to go back to my partner's house.

If you are afraid to do something, this communicates to you that approaching with courage is your path of least resistance. You likely won't be able to make much sense of this until some time passes. It's ok if you can't immediately shift fears into play, remember, you can never go wrong and there will always be more doors and opportunities. Just keep practicing.

Just as there are many varied activities of flow that one can tap into, play is the same. What gets you into a state of play is unique and different for everyone.

For me, I find going in the waves of the ocean, sitting on a swing set and kicking my legs back, listening to comedy, and playing with my children are all activities that help me get into this high alchemy state.

Doing things outside of your comfort zone, things that scare you even, are effective ways to place the vibrations of play and courage within yourself.

Again, we are capable of placing this state within our bodies without actually needing to do anything other than use our imagination. Our nervous systems cannot differentiate between an emotional response caused by outside circumstances or one caused by our imaginations.[3]

Exercise: Transmute Play

Test the theory that your imagination can naturally place you in a high alchemy state without external help.

Find a comfortable position and close your eyes. For two minutes, focus on a moment when you experienced a sense of playfulness, a time when you engaged in a new activity or faced your fears. See if you can bring the feeling of play into your body.

Can you remember a time when you or someone else did something so funny that you nearly peed your pants from laughter? Can you see the event happen again like when you first experienced it? Can you bring a smile to your own face?

My all-time experience to go back to is a memory of my partner and I trying to hike up a muddy hill. Our feet were sliding just as if on slippery quicksand as we tried to hold on to bushes covered in thorns. Seeing the look on his face, his legs spread apart as if to slide into the splits, with panic on his face, always makes me laugh.

If you struggle to think of a memory, imagine a virtual world where you are in play, and where you have located the version of You 2.0 in play. Step into their perspective and body. What does that feel like?

If you are living in deep fear and anxiety, you'll want to keep repeating this exercise every day to teach yourself what play and courage feel like once more. Once you teach yourself the sensation, reality will have no choice but to come and play ball.

Love

Love, it is said, is the driving force of this universe, the cosmos to the chaos, the yin to the yang.

In 2010, researchers discovered that the feeling of love acts as pain relief, similar to painkillers and illicit drugs like cocaine and opioids.[4] The key site in our brains for love-induced analgesia is the nucleus accumbens. This region tells the brain that you really need to keep doing whatever you are doing. Opioids essentially mimic the chemical response of the state of love. Love is the antidote to its dual pain.

The desire and need to feel loved is one intrinsic to humans. We will move mountains for it but most of us have been taught and told that love is something found outside of ourselves, through brotherhoods, sisterhoods, family, lovers, partners, children, friendships, etc. And we become depraved when we feel disconnected from this source of love because it is the true root of our creative cores.

Love can be felt as a sensation of awe, wonder, worthiness, presence, gratitude, and appreciation in the body. Love is a high alchemy state and is powerful enough to shift your focus away from red light synaptic perceptions. When you fall in love, it feels like you have no problems. When you are in awe sitting under the stars, you gain perspective over the existing chaos. It makes you resilient to red light and feels good in the body because it tells you that you are locked into your creative core.

Of all the magical words there are that the alchemist could utter, the most powerful are "thank you".

Research suggests that gratitude is not simply a cultural construct but that it has deep roots embedded in our evolutionary history, our brains and DNA, and that a grateful disposition not only leads to better health but also counteracts materialism and protects against burnout.[5]

Finding gratitude for present circumstances is the fastest way to alter our realities. When we look around at the areas where we do not have what we seek or experience dysfunction it is always because we lack gratitude around the matter.

When I no longer felt creatively inspired and I mapped out revenue targets month after month that seemed to slip through my hands, I was ungrateful for all that I had already delivered to myself, for the growths I had already conquered and undertaken. Instead I became lonely, anxious, without confidence and not enough. The revenues weren't good enough, the team wasn't good enough, I wasn't good enough. Everything became a yardstick from which I measured myself from. It was no wonder things started to spiral downwards.

Perceiving our circumstances through such a lens immediately disconnects us from the high alchemy state of love and – on the flipside – authentically compelling ourselves back into this resonance is easiest done through gratitude.

These days, I give as much thanks as often as I can, and I ensure that when I do so it is felt genuinely within my core.

Exercise: Gratitude Ritual

Again, this is an exercise of unconditional wellbeing – by teaching ourselves the calibration of this powerful force of creation: love.

Upon waking write out a list of the ten things you are grateful for in your life. This could be across health, money, relationships, family, living conditions, friendships, and even the weather.

You may at first struggle to think of ten things, especially if you find yourself in deep reds, however, as you begin to write these down you'll find more will start coming to mind. As you write each item down, repeat the words "thank you" out loud and find the resonance of genuine appreciation within your body.

The religious ritual of saying grace before a meal is a beautiful one as it places us into this space of pure love. Before consuming food or drink, take a moment to feel appreciation for the vast meal options you have, how far the produce would have had to travel to come to your table, how there is an abundance of food available to you, and how this food and drink helps to power your body with energy.

The more we give thanks, the easier this calibration is to fall into and maintain.

22

THE ETHICS OF MAGIC

We have explored the creative energies of the universe and how the human core is deeply rooted within this process.

We have also explored the forces of chaos and cosmos and how the path of least resistance works through both and that it is possible to minimize the requirement for chaos as a force when we intentionally step into our creative core.

We also understand the red light and green light system and how we should avoid conjuring for specific outcomes when we are not grounded in green.

Following this system instills ethics and integrity of our magical practice and ensures that our powers are used responsibly and to benefit all those around us. When we misuse magic to harm others, we will only hurt ourselves.

The intent, at the end of the day, is always to navigate a path of least resistance to a desired state of being:

- Freedom

- Confidence
- Love
- Joy
- Gratitude
- Flow
- Play
- Clarity
- Peace of mind

These are the things we ultimately desire.

The alchemist is the one who locks into this pathway by first validating this state before their reality even does. This is achieved through the strengthening of imagination to foster flexibility in perspectives.

Intentionally working with magic, therefore, requires the wisdom of the heart, of our own internal navigational system, and a pure alignment to love.

The Magician's Pledge

As helpful rules of thumb, here is the pledge used inside the private coven to ensure magic works for the greater good of all involved:

I will not conjure against others or to try to change others' will…

I will not conjure while in red light (unless it is purely to get back into green)...

Another's success never minimizes my own…

I am pliable in my perspective and willing to be proven wrong…I have empathy and am able to see through other points of view...

I am mindful in my use of resources for conjurings and spells…

The universe is abundant and benevolent, life is happening for me…

23

BURIAL

We are back in lockdowns, another wave, or so they tell us on the news.

I fumble with the big orange suitcase as I pull it down from the closet and lug its heavy weight onto the bed.

Unzipping it to reveal the helium tank tucked between clothes and the suicide letters I'd written a year earlier stuffed into the side pocket.

It didn't seem so menacing in the daylight, but I knew how it had been used before.

I pull out the letters, fold and tuck them into my back pocket, and lift out the tank. Shadows play over my face.

A year after the last time I'd used it, here I was pulling it back out.

Do you know what ancient humans used to call plants? My spirit guide had asked me on the astral plane of twisted willows and lavender fields.

Everything had felt like a kaleidoscope, the strange turtle creature shapeshifting as if a glitched channel. One minute it was my familiar spirit guide; the next, a monster. The monster. Something made of nightmares, curling a talon towards me and a breath on my neck.

Gods. The creature had said flatly. *That's what they called us.*

I wished to scream but the sound lodged itself like a silly-putty to the roof of my mouth and I was aware that if I did, the monster would run away.

The small room had been glowing in octarine, or maybe those had been stars. My vision had felt blurred, my legs and head heavy, a sensation that my stomach wished to hurl its contents.

The monster's breath had been upon me, I couldn't move and felt pinned down, ledden. It had wrapped a talon around my hair and green blue scales shivered as it glided past me, a cold body pressed against mine.

Look, it had said, pulling my gaze towards the center of the room. It seemed sullen and moved slower than before.

Look into the cauldron. The monster urged.

I had wanted to resist it, make a stand but I was hypnotized. My eyes moved mechanically and obediently towards the swirling light where I saw the foggy image of the willow materialize.

Am I alive?

The scene unfolded and the willow morphed into my own body, leaves turned into fingers and the twigs the limbs of flesh.

Sprawled and gasping. Just as I was the night I tried to take my own life.

I wanted to pick myself up, cradle myself in my own arms, and wipe up all the red, all the hurt and brutalities of my past. But my body was cold and lifeless, dead. Just like the willow cuttings, bled out and replete of even the beat of a heart.

I saw the bacteria multiplying, and my skin decomposing.

The skin that had pulled back from my face, revealing eyeballs in a skull and gleaming white bones transforming into branches and roots, sinking down into the mulch and upwards into the sky.

Detritus became a buffet for mushrooms sprouting over my limbs that were no longer my limbs but those of the mother tree. A pyramid of creatures: earthworms, slugs, snails, spiders, beetles, centipedes bacteria, copepods, protozoa – all crunched and munched at the soft woody fibers and moist cells.

I saw the underground fungal and root network, and nutrients pulled out from deep below towards the skies. Sun hitting leaves turning into oxygen.

Look, the monster had urged.

The scene continued to unfold to reveal spilled galaxy juice inside of the blackness of the hole in the trunk of the tree.

I saw the regenerative process of life and death, of chaos and cosmos, sped up as if happening in seconds, as if time was circular.

A great big loop. The ouroboros.

I saw the universe condense itself into a single particle only to explode outwards into a big bang and repeat the cycle over and over again. I watched this knowing billions of years passed in a matter of moments.

Spiraling galaxies swirled outwards, dark nothingness freckled in burning stars. Vibrating particles and water turning to mist.

Expansion and contraction, death and life, a big cycling, and recycling.

There was a sensation that death was an important part of this process. A knowing.

Everything is a figure eight, the monster had told me.

It showed me a collective memory.

It showed me the waltz of life.

Who are you? I had asked the monster.

It blinked and responded only:

Life.

And you are me and I am you.

And we will hold each other here.

I had reached out to touch the creature and it did not flinch. When my hand fell on the cold scales, the illusion suddenly dropped. The linen robes and monstrous expressions melted away to reveal a contorted body flanked in scars. The black eyes turned blue, and the dreadlocks became straight blond hair caked back and dirty. The beak morphed into dry lips.

I gasped and stepped back in shock.

Monster.

It blinked back at me as if hearing its name for the first time. A wheezing as it breathed hot air in the small space, a purring.

The words flashed back from the night sitting in my drug dealer's car

'Everything is a mirror.' he had told me.

The shaman, the creature, the blinking monster in front of me. The shadows that lurked. The crooked old willow in my yard.

We stared at each other suspended in time, both too afraid to make the first move.

I noticed scars across what appeared to be the wrists of the monster.

It was injured, bleeding. I saw how tired and weary it was.

A sadness overcame me. What had I done?

All along I had thought I was the victim, but now, for the first time, it was clear to me that I had been the one killing me all along.

Mirrors.

I was the monster, and the monster was me.

My hand went to its chest. *Hush now*, I had told it. *Do not be afraid. You are safe, I will take care of us both.*

Or maybe it was the monster that had said this to me. There were so many reflections it was hard to tell.

I saw the tree of life that is the willow that is me that is the monster that is a she.

And I knew what needed to be done.

So here I was now, hauling the tank from storage.

A fun fact about helium is that it is predicted that the world will run out of the natural gas in less than fifty years. I was carrying precious cargo and the tank was heavy enough to let me know there was enough of it still to accomplish the task at hand.

I walked over to the kitchen and placed it on the table. It could wait here for a moment; there was something else I needed to do first.

The weather had turned to gales. As I stepped outside, the rain came down in sheets and made my hair stick to my cheek. I wrapped my coat around myself, suicide letters firmly in hand.

The home's lights pixelate against the rain.

I steadied my gaze against the slope ahead and crossed my arms to shelter from the cold and to keep my precious cargo safe. The willow bent and swooped in the wind, which sent the wheelie bins chomping at nothing. The stream running through the property was engorged and running thick and strong. I kneeled next to the tall willow and began to carve out the soil near its base with my bare hands, dirt caking my feet. Lightning in my chest.

The suicide letters were already wet at the edges, with blue ink bleeding from the rain and my poor attempts to protect them.

I dug out a small hole in the ground, piling up the muddy dirt next to it. Within moments, my nails were crusted in black soil and the letters were reduced to soft, soggy sheets. I placed them in the hole, creating a makeshift grave. I remember the day I wrote them and the attempts I had made to end my life.

It all feels so long ago now.

I took moment to feel the magnitude of it all.

Hurrying back indoors, wrapping my arms around myself to stave off the cold, my daughter eagerly waited for me on the doorstep. She bounced up and down as if she needed to pee, her hair in ponytails and front teeth missing. Today was her birthday, and even though the lockdowns had meant no party, she was eager to open her presents, and the wait was becoming too much for a six-year-old.

"Can we do it now?" she asked. She didn't wait for me to respond, making a beeline straight to the helium tank on the table where different colored balloons were strewn next to it.

She grabbed a red balloon and pulled it over the lip of the tank, the same lip that had once been connected to a CPAP mask and a suicide bag. The balloon inflated and I helped her tie off the end.

We spent the rest of the afternoon using up the rest of the precious gas to decorate the house.

The words repeating themselves in my head:

I desire to live.

CONCLUSION: MEASURING SUCCESS

It's difficult for me to put into words why it is that I believe in magic…

…Without first talking about the monster that existed in my head.

…Without mentioning the divine timing of a knock at my door and the black mirror that showed up.

…Without telling you about how I had lost hope and the sign in the bookstore the day I resigned from my company.

How do you measure this?

Its meaning is only really significant to its perceiver.

Magic cannot be explained in such a linear fashion, making it easy to discount and brush off as coincidental.

But all around us, we are guiding ourselves, showing ourselves how to remember who we truly are. The ouroboros of life is this continual remembering and forgetting, life and death, destruction and creation.

As I have come to discover in my exploration, magic has little to do with cloaks, pointy hats, spirits, and cursed amulets. Instead, it has everything to do with the human vessel, or as the poet Novalis says, magic is "the art of consciously influencing the inner worlds."

It is about the words we use to plant seeds in our realities and enchant ourselves through. It is the stories we tell about ourselves and others throughout our lives. It is about the signal we emit and the meaning we make from it all.

It is that "something else" a person brings to what they do, an aura that compels those around them into their own cores.

From the billions of sea sparkles that light the ocean in the blue luminescence of the celestial sky above to the electrons spinning around the atom, magic permeates all parts of our realities.

We cannot escape it even if we deny its existence.

We are always in the creative act of magic, whether we know it or not.

As you continue to explore and journey down the road of alchemy, remember to continuously look for and perceive octarine – in yourself and others. Follow your nose and always question your own perceptions. Begin to collect the evidence. Spot it first in opportunities, random synchronicities, and coincidences that reek of fate. Assign meaning where it is useful to do so, leave out all the rest.

Remember that everyone's journey is different. While you may not notice results from your conjurings immediately, if you persist and keep at it, you will come to understand the true power of this practice.

Think about the work you are embarking on as the splits. If you tried to do the splits today without stretching first, you would rip some things, it would hurt and it's not advised. Same thing with magic and changing your reality.

Remember that through the chaos and cosmos, you are the alchemist. You are the creative force.

You are octarine.

You lead the way, and all that you need for the craft of reality is already within.

ENDNOTES

Introduction

1. Normandi Ellis, *Imagining the World into Existence: An ancient Egyptian Manual of Consciousness,* (Rochester: Bear & Company, 2012)
2. *Proverbs 18:21:* "Death and life are in the power of the tongue…."

3. The Chaos That Exists

1. Vishen Lakhiani, *The Buddha and the Badass: The Secret Spiritual Art of Succeeding at Work,* (New York: Rodale Books, 2020)
2. Daniel Schwemer, "*Mesopotamia,*" *Guide to the Study of Ancient Magic,* ed. D. Frankfurter (Leiden: Brill, 2019)

6. Burn at the Stake

1. Peter T. Leeson and Jacob W. Russ, *Witch Trials*, (The Economic Journal 128, 2017)
2. Leigh Alfred Walt, *The Reformation and Witch Hunts: History of Christianity*, (2019)

9. Source Code: Perspective

1. Robert Anton Wilson, *Quantum Psychology,* (Los Angeles: New Falcon Publications, 1990)
2. Dr Candace B. Pert, *Molecules of Emotion*, (New York: Simon & Schuster, 2000)
3. Stefan Klein, *We Are All Stardust: Scientists Who Shaped Our World Talk about Their Work, Their Lives, and What They Still Want to Know*, (New York: The Experiment, 2010)
4. Cameron Bailey, *The Magic of Secret Gnosis: A Theoretical Analysis of a Tibetan Buddhist "Grimoire," 2020*

13. Intent

1. The Three Initiates, *The Kybalion: A Study of Hermetic Philosophy of Ancient Egypt and Greece*

14. Source Code: Red/Green

1. Dr Candace B. Pert, *Molecules of Emotion*, (New York: Simon & Schuster, 2000)
2. Dr. Joe Dispenza, *Breaking the Habit of Being Yourself:* How to Lose Your Mind and Create a New One , (Carlsbad: Hay House, Inc., 2012)
3. Antoine Bechara, *The role of emotion in decision-making: evidence from neurological patients with orbitofrontal damage,* (Brain and Cognition, 55, 2004)

15. Source Code: Imagination

1. Suzana Herculano-Houzel, *The Human Brain in Numbers: A Linearly Scaled-up Primate Brain,* (National Library of Medicine, 2009)

17. Love Life

1. Austin Osman Spare, *The Book of Pleasure: The Psychology of Ecstasy,* 2015

19. Gnosis

1. Paul Chrystal, *In Bed with Ancient Greeks, Paul Chrystal, (*Amberley Publishing; Reprint edition, 2018)
2. Brian C Muraresku; forward by Graham Hancock, *The immortality key: the secret history of the religion with no name* , (New York: St. Martin's Press, 2020)

21. Source Code: High Alchemy States

1. Nicholas M Hobson, Juliana Schroeder, Jane L Risen, Dimitris Xygalatas, Michael Inzlicht, T*he Psychology of Rituals: An Integrative Review and Process-Based Framework*, (Personal Psychology Review, 2018)
2. Jaak Panksepp, *Affective Neuroscience: The Foundations of Human and Animal Emotions (Series in Affective Science),* (New York: Oxford University Press,

2004)

3. Joe Dispenza, *Becoming Supernatural: How Common People Are Doing the Uncommon,* (New York: Hay House, Inc., 2019)
4. Jarred Younger, Arthur Aron, Sara Parke, Neil Chatterjee, Sean Mackey, *Viewing Pictures of a Romantic Partner Reduces Experimental Pain: Involvement of Neural Reward Systems,* (Plos One, *2010)*
5. Summer Allen, Ph.D., The Science of Gratitude: A white paper prepared for the John Templeton Foundation by the Greater Good Science Center at UC Berkeley, (2018)

RESOURCES

For free training and guided pathworkings, head to magicsourcecodes.com/training

You can also find upcoming workshops and in-person events or other musings on my website, cathowell.com

If you enjoyed this book it would mean the world to me if you could leave a review on Amazon or from wherever you purchased it from.

ACKNOWLEDGMENTS

For as long as I can remember, I have always aspired to write a book, to tell a story compelling enough to positively impact the world around me. As my first book to ever be published, this expression of myself is a definition and experience of magic in itself. It is an honoring of a core desire, a moment that required thousands of lessons beforehand in order to stitch the words together. It would be amiss of me to not mention those who have played a key role in all those moments leading up to and during the publication process.

To my mother for instilling creativity and belief in the pursuit of my dreams. To my father for reminding me of the honor of the outlier. To my sister and friends for holding my hands and the late-night calls during those dark times. To my team and business partners who gave me the space to create.

To my children and their gentle soft souls for keeping me on the side of life.

My work is heavily influenced by the following mentors who have guided me and shaped my world. The works of Abraham Hicks, Dr. Joe Dispenza, Jesse Elder, Dr. Dean Radin, Robert Anton Wilson and Peter Carroll.

And finally, to the amazing community of individuals around me for allowing me to show up and celebrate this new stage of my life and always inspiring me forward and to Deb Law, for helping me to bring this book to life.

Thank you.

ABOUT THE AUTHOR

Cat is the host of The Flow Protocols podcast and a multiple eight-figure mentor to visionaries and entrepreneurs. At the height of financial success but deeply depressed, she walked away from it all in order to rebuild herself. This is a recounting of how it was that magic helped her to redefine the structures in her life and to find well-being once more. You can find more of her work on her site cathowell.com. *Magic Source Codes* is her first book.

Printed in Great Britain
by Amazon

56284427R00126